Poor People's
Social Movement
Organizations

Poor People's Social Movement Organizations

The Goal Is to Win

MELVIN F. HALL

Westport, Connecticut
London

HM
281
H27
1995

Library of Congress Cataloging-in-Publication Data

Hall, Melvin F.
    Poor people's social movement organizations : the goal is to win /
Melvin F. Hall.
        p.   cm.
    Includes bibliographical references and index.
    ISBN 0–275–94704–1 (alk. paper)
    1. Social movements.   2. Collective behavior.   3. Social change.
I. Title.
    HM281.H27   1995
    303.48'4—dc20   95–6938

British Library Cataloguing in Publication Data is available.

Library of Congress Catalog Card Number: 95–6938
ISBN: 0–275–94704–1

First published in 1995

Praeger Publishers, 88 Post Road West, Westport, CT 06881
An imprint of Greenwood Publishing Group, Inc.

Printed in the United States of America

∞™

The paper used in this book complies with the
Permanent Paper Standard issued by the National
Information Standards Organization (Z39.48–1984).

10 9 8 7 6 5 4 3 2 1

Copyright Acknowledgment

The author and publisher gratefully acknowledge permission for use of the
following material:

Extracts from *IAF: 50 Years Organizing for Change* by Cynthia Perry,
Sapir Press, 1990, p. 19. Reprinted by permission of IAF and Edward T.
Chambers.

To the residents of Detroit's Cass Corridor, 1979-1986

Contents

Tables

Preface

The goal of this book is to join social movement analysis with collective action theory. To that end, I will introduce the organizational empowerment model of collective action. All social movement theories to date lack a discussion of the influence of movement organization on the tactics of an organization. Here, a national survey of social movement organizations (SMOs) is employed to develop a model of how the organizational features of the local group, competition among social movement organizations, the political setting of the organization, and organizational empowerment influence collective action style. This model will allow for testing some long-held assumptions about organizational change as well as assumptions about the efficacy of poor people who have organized to achieve change.

Inquiry into social movements has flourished during the past two decades, with various versions of resource mobilization theory dominating the field, at least from a North American vantage point. However, few projects deal with organizational structure as it relates to forms of collective action. Gamson (1990b), Staggenborg (1989), Zald and Berger (1978), Zald and Ash (1966), and Zald and Denton (1963) have initiated some theoretical analyses of SMOs from an organizational development perspective. Most of this line of reasoning draws from Weber (Gerth and Mills 1946) and Michels (1949). Many have postulated, and this research confirms, that SMOs may not conform to Michels's "iron law of oligarchy."[1] Piven and Cloward's

(1977) assertion that formalized organization is the death knell of poor people's movements is also refuted. Other case studies (e.g., Jenkins 1983) have found that organization does not necessarily lead to impotence; moreover, this study covers nearly two hundred social movement organizations, many of which use disruptive tactics to win concessions from local officials.

Students of collective action have wrestled with organizational change and maturity (Carden 1978; Hertz 1981), the rationality of action (Olson 1965; Coleman 1986b; Knoke 1990), the pressures of collective behavior (Marx and McAdam 1994), the strength of individual interests, the relationship of structure to organizational purpose (Zald and Ash 1966), and the organizational balancing act between strategy, tactics, resources, and achieving goals (Zald and McCarthy 1987b). Following a review of social movement and collective action literature, the organizational empowerment model of collective action will be elucidated. Six specific organizational variables are outlined, and hypotheses are tested with the data from a national survey of social movement organizations and interviews with movement organizers.

In Chapter 1, I review and critique four models—classical, resource mobilization, political process, and new social movements—which are used to describe social movements. The strengths and deficiencies of all are noted.

In Chapter 2, organizational features that influence the style of collective action undertaken by poor people's SMOs are identified. An organizational empowerment model of collective action is proposed and six dimensions of SMO structure are examined: size, external funding, measure of success, who chooses tactics, dues, and networks with other organizations. Data collection and methodology are explained and the variables are analyzed.

Competition between SMOs is the topic of Chapter 3. Two broad areas of competition, territorial and organizational, are defined. Territorial competition includes struggles over turf and resources, while organizational competition focuses on the recruitment of staff, leadership styles, definition of issues, training strategies, and recruitment of members.

In Chapter 4, the importance of political climate, particularly at the local level, is examined. Interviews with organizers form the foundation for a discussion of the political climate and of how the particular political milieu helps give shape to the choice of organizational tactics. Organizers reflect on the political climate—structure of local elections, race, and type of districts—in Chicago, San Antonio, Detroit, Miami, and Oakland. The response of organizations to national legislation prohibiting discrimination in home mortgage activity is used to illustrate the impact of the national political climate on SMOs.

Chapter 5 briefly describes the recent history of poor empowerment efforts and the external support for them, putting the Campaign for Human Development (CHD) into historical and institutional contexts. There is also a discussion of the dilemmas created by external support for poor empowerment efforts. I attempt to characterize the broader support structure for groups beyond that of CHD by examining the funding patterns of the CHD-supported groups.

I am grateful to Spence Limbocker and Donald White of the Campaign for Human Development for allowing me access to CHD data. All who responded to the survey and participated in interviews helped make this book possible by providing information and by educating me. Helpful reviews were offered by Richard Williams, David Hachen, Maureen Hallinan, and John McCarthy. John McCarthy and Joseph Shields collaborated on the empowerment chapter. Chapter 3 is a joint venture with Leda McIntyre Hall. Travel for the interviews was supported by the National Science Foundation and the Notre Dame Travel Grant Fund. My thanks go to Jennifer Hennigan for providing clerical assistance and making numerous telephone calls. The editorial staff at Praeger was very helpful and patient. Long walks and meandering conversations with Glen Warn helped give focus to my ideas. Football, baseball, piano lessons, and talks with Nathan and Matthew helped give focus to my life. Finally, Leda provided invaluable editing and critique. Her devotion and support are constant.

NOTE

1. Michels's argument flows from a belief that organizations move from being less to more conservative as action-related goals are displaced by organizational maintenance goals. As an organization ages, its participants develop a vested interest in maintaining it. The result is that organizations become more accommodating to the environment that they had initially hoped to alter.

1

Social Movements and Collective Action

Had every Athenian citizen been a Socrates, every Athenian assembly would still have been a mob.   —*Plato,* The Republic

Until the early 1960s, there was a dearth of sociological research in the area of collective behavior and mass movements. The earlier writings focused primarily on crowds and panics. Le Bon (1897) is typical of these early discussions of collective behavior and seems to concur with Plato's less than charitable assessment of crowd behavior. In a crowd, "the individual may be brought into such a condition that, having entirely lost his [sic] conscious personality, he [sic] obeys all the suggestions of the operator who has deprived him of it, and commits acts in utter contradiction with his [sic] character and habits" (1897, 34). Le Bon further explains that crowd conditions release deep prejudices in a person. In a crowd, "a man [sic] is no longer conscious of his acts, certain faculties are destroyed" (1897, 35).

Fortunately, the sociological community has long since emerged from the bog of despair concerning collective behavior and social movement. The change of thought is evident in the progression of terminology from mob to crowd to collective behavior, mass movement, and finally, social movement. Of course, these terms are not interchangeable, but they do show a change in perspective from a view that emphasized the irrational to one that emphasizes the more rational element of movements and movement participants.

Others (Marx and Wood 1975) have noted changes, not only in conceptions of mass movements but in the theorists themselves. Earlier writers may have been personally or professionally threatened by social change, while later spokespersons were more or less detached researchers.   According to Marx and Wood, in the 1960s and early 1970s, these detached researchers gave way to "an increasing number of more activist researchers who view the study of collective behavior as a way to encourage social change" (1975, 364).   Since 1975, there may be yet another change as the activist researchers become somewhat further removed from "street heat" and a little more familiar with the advances and advantages of quantitative methodology.

The definitions of social movements are as diverse as the movements themselves, and perhaps all models have a definition forced upon them.   Tilly identifies a social movement as "a group of people identified by their attachment to some particular set of beliefs" (1978, 9) while McCarthy and Zald focus on change in a social structure or reward distribution (1977).   For John Wilson, a social movement is "a conscious, collective, organized attempt to bring about or resist large scale change in the social order by non-institutional means" (1973, 8). Social movements are organized, to a greater or lesser degree, to give expression to concerns, fears, terrors, injustices, and certainties or uncertainties that are common to a particular group of people.   People coalesce in order to do something about such concerns, fears, or terrors.   This action may entail a sit-in or a sit-down, a parade or a march; it may be violent or nonviolent.   The movement may have far-reaching effects—or no effect—on the norms and values of a society. Zurcher and Snow (1981) note that social movements have varying degrees of drama, significance, and success, yet they are rarely bland or without controversy.   Because other definitions fail to note the central role that tactics and collective play in social movement, I propose the following definition of a social movement: *a social movement is a collection of people who organize to change their environment, improve conditions, or resist change in their environment and who act collectively to achieve organizational goals.*

The following section critiques four dominant theories of social movements: classical, resource mobilization, political process, and the new social movement approach.   All four are analyzed and evaluated, and a brief description that delineates the specific variables for each is included.   The role of collective action in each of these four theories is critiqued, and an analysis of implications for collective action is also explored.

While theories have differing degrees of explanatory and predictive power, all are woefully weak concerning analysis and the rationale for collective action. Social movements involve people acting together; thus, for the social movement literature to be more complete, an analysis of the style and type of collective action is essential. This research both initiates an outline of the impact of organization variables on social movements and begins to examine the effect of the political climate on the type of collective action undertaken. It is illogical to imagine that a single social movement typology could address issues ranging from cults to professional lobbies and from revolutions to political reform movements. Only a very sterile and general theory could account for phenomena that are so diverse. Thus, there is no singularly effective theory of social movement phenomena; all still need to proceed with more comprehensive analyses of the types and styles of collective action.

THE CLASSICAL MODEL

The classical model of social movements is not specific to any one theorist but rather is illustrative of a whole genre of literature on social movements. The model focuses on a general tendency of social movements, namely, the progression from strain to psychological disruption and then social movement. According to the theorists who are labeled as classical (Smelser 1963; Kornhauser 1959; and Turner and Killian 1957), societal strain has a direct effect on an individual's psyche. This produces a disruption that leads directly to the formation of a social movement. In his analysis of the classical model, McAdam (1982) notes that these theorists would concur on neither the type of strain nor the specific psychological state that is induced, but all would agree that the direct cause of a social movement is an *individual's* disrupted psychological state.

The structural strain may be a result of industrialization, urbanization, a rapid rise in unemployment, changes in voting patterns, or the strain of status incongruence. Gusfield (1963) postulates that disciples of the temperance movement (which was not really a temperance movement but rather an abstinence movement) were motivated as much or more by their status incongruence as by their conviction that drink was the "devil's dishwater." He theorized that the temperance movement was a function of (1) a New England elite that was threatened by a wave of immigrants, (2) Protestants who were alarmed at the rise in the Catholic population, and (3) rural leaders who were fearful of the growing power of the urban center.

Similarly, status incongruence might be promoted as a reason why middle-class blacks joined the National Association for the Advancement of Colored People (NAACP) and Urban League in the 1940s and 1950s. These individuals experienced a gross discrepancy in being well educated and having a measure of financial success yet finding themselves relegated to second-class status. Thus, status incongruence can be seen as a structural strain that leads various factions to movement participation in an effort to ameliorate the incongruence (Geschwender 1967).

The other strains or diversions from "normal" societal functions (discussed previously) can also produce social movements. Kornhauser (1959) views the absence of integrating structures as a source of strain that leads to disruption, which in turn causes a social movement to form. Smelser uses the term generalized beliefs to refer to the disruptive psychological component of collective behavior:

These [generalized] beliefs differ, however, from those which guide many other types of behavior. They involve a belief in the existence of extraordinary forces—threats, conspiracies, etc.—which are at work in the universe. They also involve an assessment of the extraordinary consequences which will follow if the collective attempt to reconstitute social action is successful. The beliefs on which collective behavior is based are thus akin to *magical beliefs* (emphasis added). (1963, 8)

Some authors (e.g., McAdam 1982) have theorized that undergirding the classical model is the pluralist model of political power. Dahl's (1967) assumptions about widely dispersed political power may have paved the way for viewing social movement participants as psychologically dysfunctional. Because everyone has access to political power (so the theory indicates) there should be neither political nor tactical reasons to resort to social movements or collective behavior.

Critique

While this model was at the forefront of the social movement literature from 1955 to the mid-1970s, many of its weaknesses recently have become apparent. The primary cause of social movements in this paradigm is structural strain. However, it is clear that strain is omnipresent in any society, although it may fluctuate in degree. Moreover, this model fails to indicate when a strain threshold is reached that will induce a social movement. John Wilson reports that "societies are rarely stable and the forces which have the potential of producing social movements are always present in some degree" (1973, 55). If strain is always present to one degree or another, then the model does not predict at what magnitude this strain will induce a disruptive psychological state.

The overt implication of this model is that movement participants are, at best, psychologically different from non-participants. The latent implication is that participants are psychologically warped. For some individuals who adhere to this model, movement participation is not so much a way to alleviate grievances as a therapeutic exercise. People participate in order to feel better about themselves: to ameliorate a noxious psychological state.

This model also portrays movement participation as an individual exercise, which may be devoid of political meaning or purpose. This may be connected to pluralist political tendencies (as discussed previously); however, for whatever reason, social movements are analyzed on the individual level rather than in the broader political arena. McAdam writes that in the classical model "the implication is clear: the political content of the movement is little more than a conventional justification for what is at root a psychological phenomenon" (1982, 17).

Finally, the classical theorists offer very little organizational analysis. There is no indication that collective action is anything more than a therapeutic exercise for individuals, and there is no mention of the political efficacy of collective action choices or the change in forms of action that may signal organizational development. Furthermore, classical writers do not wrestle with the ways in which the changing political climate may influence the type and style of collective action. However, this classical approach has many more shortcomings than simply the lacuna concerning type and style of collective action. While recently, social psychological variables have again been touted (Gamson 1990a; Melucci 1989) as variables in the social movement equation, the notion of a movement analysis that is devoid of organizational factors and political agendas is nearly dead. The lack of analysis concerning collective action and its implications is merely another nail in the coffin.

RESOURCE MOBILIZATION

Resource mobilization has been the dominant paradigm in social movement theory for the past 15 years. The proponents of resource mobilization, like the disciples of the classical view, see structural strain as a cause of social movements; however, they view it as a necessary, but not a sufficient, cause. McCarthy and Zald (1977) would concur with John Wilson (1973), who postulates that grievances are relatively constant and pervasive. Elsewhere, writers (McCarthy and Zald 1977; Rose 1967) have noted that grievances can be manipulated or even contrived. According to this model, strain leads to discontent, from which grievances result, yet the movement will remain dormant until resources are infused. Jenkins and Perrow note that the variation "giving rise to insurgency is the amount of social resources available to unorganized but aggrieved groups, making it possible to launch an organized demand for change" (1977, 250). A major thesis of this model is that not only are resources not necessary, they almost always come from outside the aggrieved group. This infusion of resources from the outside leads to a social movement organization. From this perspective, while workers are always discontented and have numerous grievances, it is not until an outside actor provides resources that a movement will be generated and an organization formed.

Resource mobilization theorists (McCarthy and Zald 1977; Zald and Ash 1966) have noted the importance of distinguishing between a *social movement* and a *social movement organization*. While there are diverse definitions of a *social movement* (SM), the elements that are common in all definitions include: (1) goals—all social movements intend to resist or promote some kind of change; (2) people power—people join together to do the resisting and promoting; and (3) action—the people sit in, stand up, cross over, strike, resist, retreat, march, kneel, lobby, telephone, canvass, and vote.

A *social movement organization* (SMO) is a "complex, or formal, organization that identifies its goals with the preferences of a social movement or a countermovement and attempts to implement those goals" (McCarthy and Zald 1977, 12). The peace movement is composed of many segments of the population that want, work for, and promote peace. Nonetheless, there are numerous peace movement organizations (SMOs) such as the National Committee for a Sane Nuclear Policy (SANE/Freeze), Fellowship of Reconciliation, and various city wide and regional peace organizations.

While the pluralist view of power is the underpinning of the classical model, McAdam (1982) notes that Mills's (1959) perspective on the role of elites within the political system informs the resource mobilization perspective. The reason why people organize is not attributable to some psychological malfunction; rather, it is because they are locked out of the political process and movement participation is a way to enter the political arena, or at least, to influence the primary actors. Tilly (1978) makes a similar argument when he explains that challengers compete to be included as members of the polity or to influence actual members. However, the implication is clear that power is *not* equally shared and, therefore, groups on the outside tend to organize to gain a share of the power.

Resource mobilization theorists contend that often, insiders provide the resources needed by the aggrieved group. White liberals giving donations to the NAACP and the Southern Christian Leadership Conference (SCLC) or the attempts by Ronald Reagan and George Bush administrations to legitomize the pro life movement are examples that tend to support this view.

In this theory, unlike the earlier social-psychological approaches, movement participants are seen as political actors, and not merely a group therapy cadre. They are also viewed as rational actors trying to promote a political agenda. Resource mobilization theorists clearly emphasize the importance of organizations in maintaining a movement and assert that movement participants (outsiders) are linked to polity members (insiders) because of the sponsorship role that insiders often play.

Critique

While this model broadens the scope of social movement research, it has serious limitations. If social movements represent "preferences for changing some elements of the societal structure or reward distribution, or both, of a society" (Zald and McCarthy 1987b, 20), why would the elite sponsors ever become involved? Why would someone on the "inside" provide resources to a person or group on the "outside" if the outside group really wanted to change societal structures?

The issue of co-optation is inherent in the resource

mobilization understanding of social movements in general and collective action in particular. It may be a precondition of support from elites or, possibly, a condition for continued support. In the resource mobilization scheme, movement leaders need to be ever wary of stipulations imposed by benefactors.

Finally, the most serious flaw in this model is that it appears to suggest that the aggrieved population is unable to sustain its own movement and requires an elite benefactor. While it is clear that often, aggrieved groups do not possess an abundance of material resources, they generally do have the capacity to withhold resources. Piven and Cloward note:

Factories are shut down when workers walk out or sit down; welfare bureaucracies are thrown into chaos when crowds demand relief; landlords may be bankrupted when tenants refuse to pay rent. In each of these cases, people cease to conform to accustomed institutional roles; they withhold their accustomed cooperation, and by doing so, cause institutional disruptions. (1977, 24)

Because movement participants are rational actors, the style of collective action may proceed along the lines of a cost-benefit analysis. How will authorities respond? How will other SMOs respond? What have been the results of recent forms of collective action? All these questions must be considered before a style of collective action is chosen. Collective action, then, is a resource that must be used judiciously (Lipsky 1968). Tarrow (1988b) notes that a group's actions are conditioned by relations with other groups, the response of the authorities or elites, and the level of mobilization of the movement organization.

In the case of the Campaign for Human Development (see Chapter 5) and the numerous community organizations it funds, there is the potential for standing the co-optation argument on its head. It might be that individual organizations emphasize goals of change only for the sake of continued funding, while in reality, organizational maintenance is the primary goal. It seems that resource mobilization theory is particularly susceptible to overlooking such a variation.

Resource mobilization does not address the possible impact of resources gained from elites on the style and method of collective action. It seems entirely logical that the provider of the funds might have an influence on the level of contentiousness of collective action.

It may be that an SMO that receives a significant amount of external funding (e.g., grants, corporate sponsors, and foundations), as opposed to grass-roots fundraising (e.g., bake sales, raffles, dances, and dues), will be a bit more cautious in its choices of collective action, all other things being equal. In Donovan's (1973) account of the War On Poverty, he notes that funds were often cut when a group became involved in concrete change. McAdam (1982, 28) quotes Helfgot's (1974) study on the New York-based, government-supported community action organization: "From the MFY [Mobilization for Youth] experience it appears that government-sponsored social change efforts may be permitted only as long as they are ineffectual. Once a potential for change in power relationships becomes manifest, support is quickly revoked" (1974, 490). The goals of the funder (CHD as opposed to the Ford Foundation) may have an impact on whether an individual SMO is limited or feels constrained in its actions by the funding source. A funder may not "allow" certain types of collective action or object when certain issues, persons, or events are the target of the action. Thus, co-optation is an issue to consider when analyzing the goals of an organization as well as the actions.

For all their emphasis on organization, resource mobilization theorists seldom (except for Zald and Ash 1966) discuss the organizational development of social movements. Furthermore, the relation between organizational maturation and collective action has rarely been explored. In particular, examining the interaction between organizational features, political climate, and style of collective action will help to illumine some of the implications of accepting external funding.

A final problem of the resource mobilization theory is the confusion of resources and political opportunities. Perhaps, resource mobilization disciples can vindicate the theory by claiming political opportunity as a resource. However, such a climate is often (and, perhaps, always) outside the control of the local SMO, obliging it to react and adjust to the prevailing political winds. This climate may indeed help to shape the type and style of collective action independently of the organizational construct.

POLITICAL PROCESS MODEL

The political process model (McAdam 1982, 1989; Tilly, Tilly, and Tilly 1975) emphasizes that social movements are both political (as opposed to merely psychological) phenomenon and processual (as opposed to easily defined) developmental states. The model postulates at least three direct determinants of a social movement: political opportunities, organization, and cognitive liberation. The antecedent to these, according to McAdam (1982), is an undefined variable termed broad socioeconomic processes. Nowhere, however, does McAdam (the model's primary proponent) adequately discuss or elaborate on this nebulous, catch-all category.

The theory of institutional power that informs this model is derived from the Marxist tradition. Like the resource mobilization perspective, the political process model "rests on the fundamental assumption that wealth and power are concentrated in America in the hands of a few groups, thus depriving most people of any real influence over major decisions that affect their lives" (McAdam 1982, 36). However, unlike the resource mobilization perspective, political process proponents view excluded groups as possessing the power to topple the system. While this political leverage is rarely manifest, there remains a latent capability for the aggrieved population to discard its chains. This distinction has a two fold implication: (1) while power is primarily lodged with the few, it is not absolute; and (2) the aggrieved populace may, under some circumstances, generate and sustain mass action. This is not to say that challengers are in an enviable position. On the contrary, Tilly, Tilly, and Tilly (1975) give a pessimistic overview of the "outsiders'" chances.

The range of collective actions open to relatively powerless groups is normally very small. Its program, its form of action, its very existence are likely to be illegal, hence subject to violent repression. As a consequence, such a group chooses between taking actions which have a high probability of bringing on a violent response (but which have some chance of reaching the group's goals) and taking no action at all (thereby assuring the defeat of the group's goals). (1975, 283)

Thus, political process theorists ascribe some leverage, albeit limited, to the aggrieved population and insist that the forms of collective action depend on the political climate. We will consider the three primary variables represented in this model.

Political Opportunities

Political opportunities are strangely similar to what classical writers call structural strain. "Among the events and processes likely to prove disruptive to the status quo are wars, industrialization, international political realignments, prolonged unemployment and widespread demographic changes" (McAdam 1982, 41). However, unlike the classical model, as seen here, political opportunities give rise to a liberation and organization on the part of groups instead of simply generating a disruptive state among individuals. One example would be the mass migration of African-Americans to the North in the early 1900s, which changed electoral politics through the organized power of these new migrants (Lehman 1991). Likewise, Schwartz (1976) argues that the struggle between the aristocracy and industrial interests allowed for the rise of the Southern Farmers Alliance in the late nineteenth century in the United States. Contrary to the views of classical theorists, however, these new or expanding political processes are not sufficient to cause a movement. Also necessary is a strong organizational basis.

Organizational Strength

While change in the political climate may create an opening, an aggrieved population that is unorganized will not be able to step into the breach. In Freeman's review of the women's liberation movement, she mentions the need for a network of like-minded individuals. "Masses alone don't form movements, however discontented they may be" (1973, 794). Her thesis is that if there exists a lack of organizational skills, the movement will either remain a "local irritant or dissolve completely" (1973, 794). Likewise, in their study of miners in Chile, Petras and Zeitland (1967) point to the importance of organization when they indicate that "the miners' organizational skills and political competence, the proximity of the mines to the countryside, [and] the sharing of an exploited position enabled the miners to radicalize the Chilean countryside" (1967, 586).

Similarly, the civil rights movement in the United States was primarily a product of black churches and colleges, *not* of the charisma of Martin Luther King, Jr. It was the organizational force of the churches and later the Southern Christian Leadership Conference that drove the movement. King's charisma helped to popularize the movement and later added resources, but the movement itself was the result of the organization seizing a political opportunity. Piven and Cloward (1977) do not subscribe to either the political process model nor resource mobilization theory's emphasis on the importance of organization. Instead, they argue that organizations are the death of mass movements, especially for poor people. "Insurgency is always short-lived. Once it subsides and the people leave the streets, most of the organizations which it temporarily threw up and which elites helped to nurture simply fade away. Organizations endure, in short, by abandoning their oppositional politics" (1977, xxi). However, the civil rights movement, at least from 1953 to 1968, serves as a judgment against such pessimistic assessments of organizations.

Cognitive Liberation

The final independent variable proposed by this model is cognitive liberation. This occurs when an aggrieved people believe that something can be done to change their condition. In the language of the civil rights workers, there comes a time when you become "sick and tired of being sick and tired" (McAdam 1982). While Piven and Cloward are much more pessimistic than the political process theorists about the role of organizations, they are explicitly clear about what is here called cognitive liberation.

The emergency of a protest movement entails a transformation both of consciousness and of behavior. The system, or those aspects of the system that people experience and perceive, loses legitimacy. Large numbers of men and women who ordinarily accept the authority of their rulers and the legitimacy of institutional arrangements come to believe in some measure that these rulers and these arrangements are unjust and wrong. (1977, 3-4)

They continue by saying that at this point, people begin to assert their rights and that there arises a "new sense of efficacy" (1977, 4). People begin to believe that things actually can be changed.

The social-psychological focus of the model is obvious in this variable. The model suggests a psychological change whereby people from an aggrieved population cease to attribute their position to themselves but instead come to view their plight and that of others as the result of situational factors. It should be noted, however, that this cognitive liberation may only occur only after an accompanying expansion of political opportunities and the development of a strong organization have taken place. A "critical mass" must be reached to promote liberation.

Critique

If resource mobilization over emphasizes the importance of outside resources, this model accounts for neither their origin nor their role. It fails to answer the question, From where come the resources to sustain the movement, and in turn, the organization that fuels the movement? Do the members provide the resources, do they come from the outside, or are resources unimportant? None of these issues are addressed. McAdam, the primary promoter of this model, fails to address why strain does not always lead to political opportunities. If strain is relatively constant (Wilson 1973), why are political opportunities and movement organizations not equally so?

This model also posits that political opportunities lead to social movements. Surely, however, opportunity can be missed or ineffectively exploited because resources are scarce. There may also be an inefficient management of the issues. Perhaps resources, such as money, are part of the organizational strength variable, yet nowhere does McAdam (1982) include this factor as part of the organizational package.

The view of collective action (McAdam 1982; Tilly, Tilly, and Tilly 1975) embodied in the model seems a bit truncated as well. Are the only two choices available to challenging groups to commit violence or to acquiescence? Certainly, the history of the civil rights movement in this country, as well as of the independence movement in India, suggest that collective action can take many forms that fall between these two extremes.

The role accorded to collective action also seems minimal in this model. Is collective action not how a social movement presses its demands? Because these groups are not part of the elite few who hold power, they must use non institutional means to either gain access or get their agenda recognized. However, this model fails to analyze adequately the role that collective action plays in promoting organizational strength and developing cognitive liberation. Although Piven and Cloward could not be categorized precisely as adherents to the political process model they do hint that action forms may change as an organization develops. More specifically, as organizations form, action types become less oppositional. The absence of a discussion of collective action is surprising in light of the model's emphasis on power. Actions taken by a social movement are manifestations of power, and as organizations develop it would be interesting to note changes in action types and displays of power. While the variable of political climate or opportunity is addressed, a discussion concerning organizational variables as they relate to types of collective action is missing in this model.

NEW SOCIAL MOVEMENTS

Since the 1970s, a number of writers (primarily European) have been promoting a social movement analysis that they call *new social movements*. These new social movement researchers (Melucci, Cohen, Klandermans, Castells, Touraine, and others), who share neither methodology nor perspectives, are nevertheless unified in their belief that something is dramatically different about current (post-1965) social movements compared to earlier movements. The primary emphasis of these writers is to explore *why* social movements mobilize, largely to the exclusion of *how* movements mobilize. Thus, the emphasis is on structural issues: the structural causes of social movements, their animating ideologies, and their relations to the culture of advanced capitalist societies (Klandermans and Tarrow 1988).

To some degree, these European researchers are reacting against the legacy of Marxist analysis, in which the working class is viewed as the principal vehicle for a social movement and material benefit is the primary goal (Touraine 1981). Not unlike resource mobilization, which reacted strongly to the shortcomings of the classical approach, new social movement theory is a protest against a narrowly defined Marxist view that perceives social movements as based only on the relations of production and social class. New social movement researchers (Cohen 1985; Castells 1978; Touraine 1981) assert that old forms of social movement based on class or class consciousness are no longer applicable in a post-industrial society. The new social movements have abandoned a revolutionary dream in favor of structural reform, an approach that focuses on social relations between actors with conflicting interests. Usually, these actors are not individuals (though they may be) but groups, and the social relations are not determined by production forces.

The new social movements include environmental issues, feminist issues, gay rights, reproductive issues, and anti-nuclear issues. These movements do not have the overthrow of a polity as their goal but rather want to have their issue introduced for discussion by the polity. Melucci (1989) reports that problems of the "limits of the system" lead to both economic strife and political confrontation. New social movements, according to Klandermans (1986), are primarily single-issue groups that are contenders inside the polity. Touraine (1984) calls them actors fighting for the social control of historicity, by which he means cultural, economic and ethical modes within a society. Castells (1983) writes that new urban social movements come about when organizations try to move a neighborhood from a profit (commodity) approach to more of a use-value focus. Certainly, the proliferation of worker cooperatives in the Basque region of Spain is an example of a change to a use-value orientation. These cooperatives are not only just small shops and factories but also include doctors, hospitals, and retail outlets. Various worker cooperatives in the United States that sprang from the Congress for a Working America in Milwaukee, Wisconsin, would also fit Castells's use-value approach. Moreover, Castells (1983) suggests that when a particular minority tries to carve out a section of a city or neighborhood and change its orientation, it exemplifies a new social movement. He cites as evidence gays in San Francisco who planned which neighborhoods in the city to claim as their own, based on the type of bars and available housing.

Klandermans and Tarrow (1988) and Klandermans (1984) list four ways in which new social movements differ from the old.

1. Values: new social movements are usually antimodernistic. For them, bigger is not always better, and they reject the premise that society is based on economic growth. Anti-nuclear protests as well as environmental actions point to a new or different set of animating values.

2. Action forms: often, new social movements make use of

unconventional forms of action. These groups also tend to favor small, decentralized organizations.

3. Constituency: the constituency of these new social movements is twofold, consisting of individuals who are directly (adversely) affected by modernization and those who are sensitive to problems resulting from modernization, and particularly newly, well-educated individuals from upper and middle-class backgrounds.

4. New aspirations: since these new actors have been assured of material satisfaction, they develop non-material needs such as self-actualization and participation.

According to Klandermans (1986) and Cohen (1985), these four aspects differentiate new social movements from the old. However, are these emphases qualitatively different from the resource mobilization approach? Moreover, what is the influence of organization on these values and aspirations? What types of collective actions display these new values, and are the actions different from those of previous movements?

We have seen that the pluralist understanding of democracy was one of the cornerstones of the classical model of social movements, just as an elitist perspective informs resource mobilization theory and a Marxist approach is embodied in the political process model. New social movement theorists rely heavily on Habermas's (1975) understanding of the role of the state as their theoretical linchpin. "The intervention of the state and capitalistic economy into the new reaches of life is the chief explanation for the use of new social movements" (Klandermans and Tarrow 1988, 16). Habermas (1975, 1984) emphasizes the state's encroachment into personal lives in, for instance, reproductive rights and the symbiotic relationships between the state and capitalistic economy, such as tax abatements and corporate bailouts. Because of these encroachments, actors (groups) seek to establish space between themselves and the state. Cohen (1985) emphasizes that these new social movements are self-limiting in that they neither seek nor maintain commitment based on equal power but rather limit themselves to the defense and extension of spaces for social autonomy. Neither do the new social movements want to overthrow the democratic state or the market economy; rather, they seek to carve out a space or a redrawing of the boundaries between the public and private realms.

In summary, new social movements are endemic to industrialized and post-industrial societies. As groups seek either to gain space or maintain an identity, they confront the polity with various types of collective actions. They want to reorganize the relation of economy, state, and individual or to redraw boundaries between social sectors. Many actors interpret their actions as attempts to renew a democratic political culture, and not to overthrow a polity. These groups are generally oriented toward a single issue and cut across social and economic boundaries.

Critique

Like many theories that are a corrective to a previously popular paradigm, the theory of new social movements researchers has filled a gap in social movement research. The analysis of post-modern, post-industrial society and the connection with social movements constitute one of the strengths of this theory. Brand's (1985) classification of new social movements as focusing on rising demands or need defense is instructive. Rising demands produce new values and needs that directly conflict with the traditional value system. Need defense movements, such as reproductive rights, point out the negative consequences of modernization for the individual. Such analysis moves social movement theory away from class struggle and meta-social causes. Some researchers (Touraine 1983) emphasize the ability of people to act in their given historical context, rejecting both a structuralist and a deterministic view of history. History is what people make it, according to the new social movement theorists. Touraine (1983) in particular flatly rejects Lenin's oft-repeated dictum that workers can only reveal and aggravate constraints without being able to escape their chains.

While there is not unanimity (Touraine is one exception), new social movement theorists have reintroduced social psychology to the social movement field. As a result, Gamson writes, "Social psychology bashing among students of social movements is over (1990a, 1). The emphasis in new social movements on values, identity, and micro-mobilization is a corrective to resource mobilization which stated that "grievances and discontent may be defined, created, and manipulated by issue entrepreneurs and organizations" (McCarthy and Zald 1977, 1215). For new social movements, the values of the post-modern society are important and grievances arise from a market economy, which can, and does, fuel social movements. The new social movements approach, with its affinity for social-psychological interpretations, has helped to redefine what it means for a social movement to be successful. For Melucci (1989), a collective identity is not merely instrumental to the success of a collective action, that collective identity itself is a goal of movements. Melucci argues against "an exclusively political view centered on the 'instrumental' dimension of action" because it treats "as 'expressive' or residual the self-selective investments of the movements" (1989, 73-74). Success, then, is not always defined in the outcome of the collective action but rather in the formation of the collective identity that leads to the action. This aspect of collective action is conspicuously absent in the resource mobilization literature.

There are, however, some troubling elements in new social movement theory. It seems to divert attention away from the political process of the movement and fails to confront how organizations are formed, how grievances are connected to collective action, and how organization structure affects the type and form of collective action. In addition, the theory's description of participants as individuals adversely affected by modernization or a market economy, along with other well-educated individuals who are sensitive to these developments, seems strangely similar to accounts from resource mobilization theory about the aggrieved group and outside elites who provide funding.

New social movement theorists (Klandermans and Tarrow 1988) also emphasize new inventive forms of collective action without specifying what these are. Are they forms of civil disobedience? These have been used for years by movements in both modern and less developed countries. Are these new forms of action staged by the media? Recall the Boston Tea Party and Mohandas Gandhi's march to the sea; clearly, this form has been used for a long time.

An emphasis on decentralized organizations and a single-issue focus are also considered to form a cornerstone of the new social movements (Klandermans and Tarrow 1988); however, organizations such as Greenpeace are highly and rigidly organized. Likewise, Castells's (1983) analysis of the gay community in San Francisco revealed that gays were not only interested in creating living space but also pressured city government for open housing reforms. Rather than being minimally organized, they were so politically astute and organizationally effective that they have been influential in a number of mayoral races in San Francisco. The same may be said for the Greens in Germany, who are now a force in German national elections. Clearly, these are not small-scale, anti-bureaucratic groups.

Finally, although Melucci (1989) and other new social movement theorists in general have helped to redefine success to include collective identity, no group will survive if collective action is not efficacious—no matter how intense the collective identity. This emphasis, along with Inglehart's (1971) focus on self-actualization, comes precariously close to the classical theory's overemphasis on the psychological needs of movement participants.

As was true of the other theories examined previously, new social movement theory omits any analysis of action types or collective action styles. Why do some organizations choose contentious forms of collective action while others prefer a less confrontational type? How does organization development contribute to these choices of collective action? By their own admission (Klandermans and Tarrow 1988), new social movement theorists have focused on *why* a social movement exists, but not *how* it forms.

CONCLUSION

The goal of this review is not to elevate one theory and discredit others but to review the strengths and weaknesses of each. Obviously, some of the typologies are more robust, and thus more useful, than others. The shortcomings of the classical, or "hearts and minds," approach are obvious and imposing. However, some cult-like movements may be lodged in individualized compartments as the hearts and minds approach provides.

The political process model is an extension of the resource mobilization model, and as such, it does include social psychology (cognitive liberation) in its equation. However, if resource mobilization overestimates the role of outsiders by way of resources, political process seems to undervalue the importance of resources in maintaining a movement. New social movement theory gives the researcher a different set of tools than either political process or resource mobilization. New social movement writers are primarily interested in *why*, and not *how*, a movement originates. The new social movement approach is to ask different questions than those of either resource mobilization or political process adherents.

The shortcomings and pitfalls of resource mobilization have been well documented. Foremost among these is co-optation, loose definition of resources, and a refusal to acknowledge the role of social psychology. Nonetheless, its explanatory power remains strong in this era of movement entrepreneurs and corporate funding. The co-optation argument may fall if the funding agency has social change or empowerment as its goal. Certainly, some tightening of the definition of resources is needed.

What all models lack is the ability to explain the type of collective action a group employs. Why among groups with essentially the same goals, do some march while others negotiate? Why do some only write letters while others lobby and still others use direct action? How do groups that use all these tactics (and more) decide what form to use? Finally, and most important to this study, what is the organizational construct that undergirds such decisions?

What is of interest to this study is not how or why a movement emerges, but rather the organizational determinants and political climate that shape the type of collective action a functioning social movement organization displays. I am proposing that a model that includes organizational maintenance, internal polity, goals, and inter-organizational relations will give shape to organizational tactics. Specifically, variables such as age and size of the organization, percentage of external funding, organizational purpose and goals, level of democracy, and size and scope of organizational networks have a significant influence on the style and type of collective action's that are chosen. In addition to these organizational characteristics, the concept of political climate (both local and national) is introduced as an important variable for consideration.

2

Getting to the Table

The whole history of the progress of human liberty shows that concessions yet made to her august claims have been born of earnest struggle. If there is no struggle there is no progress.

—*Frederick Douglas*

In March, 1981, the tenants of 437 and 439 Charlotte, both three-story, fifty-unit buildings in the middle of Detroit's poorest and most populated neighborhood, were relieved when they received the following letter: "Despite the rumors that you have been hearing, Renaissance Reality has no intention of selling the building to the Masonic Temple or any other group. We encourage you to stay in the building and even invite your friends to consider renting one of the ten vacant apartments." The residents, most of whom were elderly or living near the poverty line, immediately conveyed this information to the local community organization, the Concerned Citizens of the Cass Corridor (4Cs), a group that had been concerned about the Masonic Temple's interest in the buildings surrounding its structure. The community organization had heard that the Temple was interested in buying these two buildings and four others on Charlotte and Second Streets in order to expand their parking lot. Members of the 4Cs development committee had made some initial inquiries with the Temple and their real estate personnel and been told there were no plans to purchase the buildings on Charlotte or other apartment buildings on nearby Second Street. The members of the 4Cs were concerned because of the recent rash of condominium conversions and the demolition of housing for low- and moderate-income residents. Ninety-eight percent of the people in the neighborhood lived in apartments, and 60% of them were at or below the poverty line, so there was much relief when the owner indicated he was not selling the buildings. A few of the tenants had recently moved to 437 and 439 Charlotte after being evicted from other buildings that been converted to condominiums or demolished. Others had lived in the buildings for a long time; the average length of residence was 13 years.

On April 12, the residents received another communication from the buildings' owners: "In an effort to upgrade the neighborhood we are selling our building to the Masonic Temple. Therefore you must leave the building by May 15. We will provide you with transportation when you find a new apartment." The entire community was outraged. They found it more than ironic that six weeks earlier, the owner had promised the building would not be demolished and had even exhorted the residents to encourage their friends to move in. Now, they were being evicted to "upgrade the neighborhood," a cruel euphemism for the construction of a parking lot. Countless meetings ensued, with the residents asking for the Temple to consider other alternatives, including a parking structure on the vacant land across the street. During these meetings, it became clear that other buildings were on the Masonic "hit list" as well.

The community organization decided to hold a public demonstration at the Masonic Temple at the opening performance of the visiting New York Metropolitan Opera. Opening night arrived, and Detroit's finest dressed citizens were greeted by 300 residents of the neighborhood, some of them in wheelchairs. The residents distributed leaflets that quoted the two letters and outlined the alternative parking possibilities. All four television stations covered the event, as did both the daily newspapers. Despite such attention, the Temple went on with the eviction, and by mid-June, all the tenants had left except Frank Alberts. Alberts, a Native American who was a veteran of the Korean War (he said as a result of the war his hearing was diminished and he could no longer hear the birds sing) decided he would not move. He claimed he was tired of being moved out of buildings to "upgrade" the neighborhood, tired of "doing the Corridor shuffle," as he called it. For three months, Frank lived alone in the building, the final two without electricity. Frank was supported by other members of the 4Cs, who took him food and went to his aid during a rash of vandalism and fires that occurred during his solitary stay in 437 Charlotte. Frank said he wanted to force the Temple to negotiate with the community organization over the future of the rest of the buildings. Finally, the Masonic Temple representatives agreed to meet with the 4Cs and subsequently promised not to purchase and demolish any more buildings. Two of the other buildings on the block were purchased by the community group and turned into housing cooperatives. The original two buildings were razed and the parking lot was expanded; however, the other buildings were saved.

The influence of organizational structures and operating procedures on the types of actions in which social movement organizations engage has not been systematically investigated. The types of actions often include intensive letter writing campaigns, public debates, informational pickets, accountability sessions, public demonstrations, acts of civil disobedience, and occasionally violence. A few researchers (Gamson 1990b; Staggenborg 1989; Zald and Ash 1966) initiated some theoretical analyses of the social movement organization (SMO) from an organizational development perspective. Others, who are particularly interested in poor people's organizations (Barnes 1987; Jenkins 1985b; Hertz 1981), note that organizational change or maturity does not inevitably proceed in the direction of greater bureaucratization. There is considerable debate concerning the change of actions, by SMOs in general and poor people's organizations in particular, and the waning of an issue (Gamson 1990b; Goldstone 1980). Organizational ecology researchers notice the link between organizational age and failure rates as well as note the liabilities of new movement organizations (Conell and Voss 1990; Hannan and Freeman 1989).

In this work six hypotheses concerning the relationship between organizational structure and tactical decisions are tested using multiple regression and structured interviews with members of the organizations. This approach does not attempt to explain why *individuals* engage in actions nor why *individuals* join social movements. Instead, the focus is on analyzing how organizational characteristics contribute to the style of action. The goal is to offer an alternative to the traditional wisdom that increases in organizational size, maturity, and external funding extend the probability of organizational quiescence (McAdam 1982; Helfgot 1974; Donovan 1973). The failure to consider the influence of organizational structure on tactics is a shortcoming of all major social movement theories.

This chapter extends research on social movements and poor people's organizations in three ways. First, it challenges Piven and Cloward's (1977) assertion that formalized organization is the death knell of poor people's movements. They contend that when poor people's movements try to build an organization, they spend energy doing that which they *do not* do well—build an organization—often at the cost of failing to do what they *can do* well—disrupt, obstruct, and escalate tension. This work includes 187 poor people's social movement organizations, many of which have used disruptive tactics to win concessions from local officials. Piven and Cloward's study of the civil rights, labor, and the welfare rights movements led them to conclude that organizational concerns commence the slide down the slippery slope toward movement demise or, worse yet, impotence. The organizations in this work are similar in many ways (with trained leaders, locally controlled, reliant on disruptive tactics, and with some dependence on external resources) to the three movements studied by Piven and Cloward, and all are part of a poor people's movement. Other researchers, using a case study approach (Valocchi 1990; Barnes 1987; Jenkins 1985b), have taken issue with the determinism of Piven and Cloward but this study extends the debate by analyzing a large number of social movement organizations.

Second, some of the organizational features that influence the style of collective action undertaken by poor people's SMOs are identified. These features include organizational maintenance, measure of organizational success, internal polity, interorganizational relations, and sources of funding. Some researchers (Buechler 1990; Zald and Ash 1966) have argued that different organizational structures are required for differing organizational purposes. However, the influence of these structures on collective action needs to be examined.

Third, this chapter furthers the discussion of the role of collective action in social movements, and particularly poor people's groups (Conell and Voss 1990; Langton 1986). Social movements inherently involve action by either an outsider trying to get in or an insider trying to keep the outsider out. Movements also involve groups trying to promote their particular agenda for political or legal consideration. Collective action refers to those events, tactics, or actions that produce a public good, and it always involves a group of people who claim to represent a larger public, agency, group, or organization (Olzak 1989). Much of the research on collective action since Olson (1965) has attempted to refute or modify his economic calculus (Gamson 1990b; Oliver and Marwell 1988). However, most of these arguments deal with the rational choice perspective which attempts to explain why *individuals* do or do not participate in collective action.

Event analysis broadens the scope of collective action from

individual rationality to include political opportunities such as analysis of the relative strength or weakness of states (Birnbaum 1988), changes in population (Piven and Cloward 1977), and changes in voting patterns (McAdam 1982). However, much of the event history analysis of collective action pertains only to the political environment of the collective action, and often it ignores the social movement organizations that drive the tactics.

Recently, an expanded version of a theory of association political economy (Knoke 1990) emerged, which seeks to focus attention on both micro and macro social levels of behavior. Once again, the primary focus ison the individual, though here it is expanded to include reciprocal relationships between the individual and the organization. Even when the focus tends toward a more social-psychological and interpretive understanding of collective action (Benford and Hunt 1992; Snow, Rochford, Worden and Benford 1986), the primary focus remains at the individual level.

Increasingly, methodological individualists and rational choice proponents (Oberschall 1993) have advocated a shift from individual to group and societal analysis. The data discussed in this chapter provide the opportunity to integrate the macro and micro levels through the development of what might be called a model of empowerment. At a more descriptive level, the chapter explores some of the actions that groups use to get the attention of decision arbiters and policy makers.

ORGANIZATIONAL EMPOWERMENT AND SIX DIMENSIONS OF SMO STRUCTURE

Most of the writing on social movement groups has focused on inevitable conservatism (Michels 1949), centralization of control (Zeitlin 1968), routinization of tasks (Wilson 1973), decrease in the use of unruly tactics (Piven and Cloward 1977), loss of control or interest by members (Wilson 1973), or the collapse of the movement because of myopic concern with building an organization (Piven and Cloward 1977). This pessimism regarding the efficacy and tenure of social movement organizations has dominated the study of poor people's movements.

I contend that there is another way of understanding poor people's organizations, namely, that they may empower people to act in such a manner that concessions are won. This alternative vision arises from several internal and external factors that may facilitate contentious actions. While this analysis does not exhaust the possible organizational causes of contentious action, the variables analyzed here were chosen because nearly all have been used as predictors of the decline or failure in poor people's movements.

As has been noted elsewhere (Delgado 1986; Jenkins 1985b; Piven and Cloward 1977), poor people often use unruly tactics. Because of alienation from the electoral system and other traditional avenues of influence, poor people may be particularly inclined toward contentious actions as a way of commanding notice in the political arena. The importance of recognizing repertoires of collective action has been part of the discussion of social movementsdiscussion for some time. Tilly (1978) argues that at any one point in time, the repertoire of available collective actions is limited. For poor people's groups, the collective action choices are severely limited and the actions that appear to work are often those that are disruptive. These choices may be organizationally driven, and certain organizational features may more readily facilitate such tactics than others. Among the internal factors that conceivably influence tactical choices are the size of the organization, organizational budget, age of the organization, dues requirement, goals of the organization, and ways in which the organization measures success.[1] External factors that, I argue, affect tactics and, therefore, organizational empowerment include interorganizational cooperation, external funding, the local political agenda, and the national and international political climate. Nearly all these internal and external factors have been discussed piecemeal in the social movement and poor people's organization literature. One of the features of the data used in this analysis is that all these variables are analyzed together. This chapter tests several of the claims concerning the way SMO structures and operating procedures inform tactical considerations, using six dimensions of SMO structure and operations.

Size

Size should influence the style of action in which a group engages. Saul Alinsky once claimed that participation by 3% of a community would ensure the success of a community organization. Other writers (Reitzes and Reitzes 1986) have noted that community organizations do not require mass participation and that a few individuals can legitimate the organization for the whole. However, it has been found that organizational mortality decreases with size (Hannan and Freeman 1989). Organizational size is a form of power, and often, organizations that can generate numbers (of members) are perceived by the ruling polity to be the most powerful. This research predicts that although mass participation may not always be necessary for the SMO to achieve recognition, larger organizations will tend to use more contentious forms of collective action. Because of this "people power," the hypothesis is that *large organizations are the most likely to use unruly tactics, such as public demonstrations, direct actions, acts of civil disobedience, or accountability sessions.* Accountability sessions are events at which a public official is invited to a community meeting and questioned about specific issues. The SMO runs the meeting in a very efficient yet confrontational style, and officials are often publicly humiliated. While on the surface, these accountability sessions may not seem to fit the mold of unruly tactics, they are nearly always threatening and embarrassing for local political elites. In many communities, local officials refuse to attend such sessions after experiencing them once because of the potential for public humiliation and the level of contentiousness.

External Funding

To my knowledge, the relationship of external funding to style of collective action has never been tested. Arguments abound concerning the effect of external funding on an organization (McAdam 1982; Jenkins 1981; Helfgot 1974; Donovan, 1973), but the *source* of the funding is rarely considered. If the goals of the funding agency are to change society and restructure power, then external funding may well induce groups to engage in more contentious forms of action. The cases of the War on Poverty programs (Donovan 1973) and the Mobilization for Youth (Helfgot 1974) are examples of the possible deleterious effects of outside funding on tactics. If the funding agency is not really interested in *structural* change, then the effect of increasing external funding is often quiescence. However, if the goals of the funding agency involve structural change, then the effect of external funding may lead to more radical goals and contentious actions on the part of the SMO. The influence of external funding on tactical decisions may not be straightforward and is likely to be minimal, particularly for poor people's organizations. Therefore, it is predicted that *for poor people's SMOs, external funding will have little or no influence on tactical contentiousness.*

Measure of Organizational Success

For this work one of the central issues concerning the focus of the organization is how the SMO measures success. What is termed success of an organization is sometimes attributed to structural or historical circumstances that are independent of the protesting group (Piven and Cloward 1977). Some writers (e.g., Staggenborg 1989) have postulated that organizational connections will influence both the style and efficacy of collective action. The most thorough account of collective action and its ultimate outcome is Gamson's (1990b) in which he finds that groups who set as a goal the displacement of an existing political figure are not likely to be successful. However, those organizations that resort to violence or unruly tactics are more likely to achieve their goals, at least partially, than are groups whose tactics are more restrained. Although organizational success is not the principal thrust of this chapter, success certainly is the focus for those who design and implement the tactics in local SMOs. In my study, each organizer was asked about the tactics of his or her organization and the goal of the actions. A West Coast organizer captured the sense of all organizers interviewed when he replied:

The goal is to win. This win is often not the final victory we work for, but every action is designed to get a response from the authorities and improve our bargaining position, in order to "get to the table" [the negotiating table]. We expect to win something every time we do an action. (October 1991)

The particular measure of success that an SMO employs will help to shape the style of collective action that is used. It is important to note that examining the measure of success that an organization employs is not the same as determining whether an organization is successful (Gamson 1990b; Goldstone 1980). The concern here is the mechanism that the organization uses to measure success.

Organizations with specific goals and measurable criteria that define success as winning on issues typically have a specific focus, whereas SMOs with more general or abstract goals, which measure success in such terms as, for example, "achieving justice," usually have a corresponding general focus. The NAACP's general focus on achieving equality for black Americans resulted in tactics that centered primarily on legal challenges, while the tactics of the Student Nonviolent Coordinating Committee (SNCC), which included, but were not limited to, lunch counter sit-ins and street demonstrations, reflected the committee's focus on achieving specific local changes. When there is a specific demand put forth—rent to be set at a certain level, a particular building to be torn down, a toxic dump site to be cleaned—contentious actions are often used. Groups that are locked out of the political process (this nearly always applies to poor people's groups) and who want to win on their particular issue are more likely to use any means necessary, short of violence in this setting, to gain victory. While it is difficult to measure the degree to which organizations are excluded from the bargaining table, the measure of success employed by the organizations is evident. Contentious tactics are often used to get the attention of the media in order to win the sympathy and support of the public, potential adherents, or bystanders (McCarthy and Zald 1977) or in order to force (or embarrass) policy makers, political leaders, and people in power into action that they would not ordinarily take. It seems safe to assume that because all these groups are initially locked out of the decision-making process, contentious actions will result. The hypothesis is that *poor people's SMOs which have specific criteria to measure success will tend to use more contentious actions than those with abstract or general goals.*

Choosing the Tactics

The internal polity of a poor people's organization also influences the way in which it relates to the external polity that it intends to influence. The level of democratization within an SMO contributes to the formation of tactical choices. Specifically, in this case the emphasis is on who makes the decisions concerning tactics. Gamson (1990b) uses bureaucratization as a determinant of both style of action and level of success. Studying groups existing from 1800 to 1945, he uses variables such as by-laws, membership lists, and a constitution to represent a level of bureaucratization. However, in the last 40 years, with the proliferation of funding agencies, virtually every organization has instituted by-laws, membership lists, and the like; consequently, there is very little variance across organizations.

The degree of centralization in decision making, although not a proxy for bureaucratization, does allow for testing whether membership control has an effect on style of action. Specifically, is there a discernible difference in the tactics of those SMOs in which members select the types of collective action and those SMOs that rely on the decisions of the leadership or staff? People who have been locked out of the broader societal decision making-process are often unfamiliar with the art of gentle negotiations and, more important, may have deep suspicions about meetings where the external polity's leaders are in control. Often, social movement organizations form because traditional tactics such as telephone calls, legal challenges, voting, meetings, and letter writing have not alleviated the grievances. *In poor people's SMOs, if the members choose the tactics, the actions will likely be more contentious.*

Dues

The requirement of dues is an indicator of "ownership," particularly in poor people's organizations. Cesar Chavez, of the United Farm Workers, insisted that members be required to pay dues, explaining: "Members commit themselves to the organization by paying dues regularly. Because they pay they feel they are part of the organization" (Delgado 1986, 86).

The requirement of annual dues for members of an organization begins to separate constituents from bystanders. A leader of a federated organization reports that his organization "lives or dies based on the membership's willingness to organize and pay their dues. If the membership stops paying dues we are out of business" (Delgado 1986, 48). For many poor people, annual dues may be more costly than contentious collective actions, which is often quite the opposite for members of more traditional interest groups or lobbying efforts. It is predicted that *those organizations which have a dues requirement will tend to engage in more contentious tactics.*

Network

Because local social movement organizations rarely exist in isolation from other SMOs, interorganizational relations are an important force in molding tactical choices. A shared identity may develop, or conversely, competition over resources may lead to non-cooperation. Social psychologists have noted the importance of the "group shift" phenomenon whereby groups that relate often with others of similar interests tend to shift more dramatically to the already preferred actions (Zuber, Crott, and Werner 1992). Because this tendency has been noted, the relationship between the quantity of interorganizational relations and the type of tactics is of concern for poor people's organizations. Other studies of organizations found that interorganizational linkages increase legitimacy (e.g., Singh, Tucker, and House 1986).

Assessing how frequently a group interacts with other organizations should reveal some of the influences of political climate on collective action. Such relations with other organizations can be used to marshal more organizational strength or at least create the illusion thereof. SMOs, like other groups that often relate to one another, will tend to polarize around more extreme tactics (LaFrance and LaFrance 1977). In this situation, there are often individuals who advocate more contentious tactics, and such zealots are often considered to be more committed to the cause. The resulting admiration may induce groups to polarize around the more contentious tactics. Such interrelationships may also result in more effective evaluation of tactics that work. It is expected that *poor people's SMOs that meet often with similarly directed organizations will be likely to engage in more unruly actions*.

These are not the only potentially significant factors that influence organizational contentiousness. The cross-sectional design used here does not allow for a test of the oligarchy hypothesis (Michels 1949), an argument that suggests that organizations become quiescent as they age. The effect of organizational age on tactical choices is not examined here.

However, the interviews lead me to believe that the history of the organization may have an influence on the types of tactics employed. A community organizer in Chicago mentioned that his organization formerly undertook many direct actions but now often needed only to threaten such actions to get the attention of the alderperson, local developers, and even the mayor. He spoke of a direct action aimed at the owner of a professional sports team who wanted to build a new stadium within the boundaries of the organization. The community organization tried to meet with the owner and develop an alternative plan to the proposed razing of a several square block area. However, the city officials, the developer, and the owner rebuffed the community's desire to participate in the plan. Continually excluded from the planning for the new stadium, the community organization decided to take its plea to the home and neighborhood of the team owner. About 200 members went to his house, played games on his lawn, urinated in the streets, and carried signs about how good a new stadium would be for his neighborhood. They also outlined all the houses, parks, and businesses that would need to be demolished to make way for the stadium. These actions received press coverage from local television stations and three newspapers. Eventually, the plan failed, although as the organizer admits, the community group's actions may not have been the only, or even the major, determinant of the outcome.

Three years later, another professional sports team wanted to construct a new stadium to replace the old one which was already located in the organization's area. This time, team officials, city representatives, and developers approached the organization asking for a meeting. Negotiations ensued, the developers agreed to build low-income housing units for displaced residents, and the community group gave its approval and cooperation to the project.

Similar scenarios were reported in interviews in Detroit, Michigan; San Antonio, Texas; Oakland and San Francisco, California; and rural Tennessee. All organizers conceded that they used less contentious forms of action than formerly, but the reasons had to do with becoming a "player" in the political game. It was mentioned that often, the mere threat of an action is sufficient, although a few organizers reported that occasionally, the actions must come to fruition in order to let the "powers that be" know that the organization retains the willpower to act. The relationship between tactical history and oligarchy cannot be explored with this design, but the anecdotal evidence encourages a consideration of organizational history as a resource. The role of the national and local political climate is also not considered here, and other organizational issues are not covered due to space limitations. Instead, this research seeks to isolate and intensively explore a few of the important organizational features and procedures that are thought to have a strong influence on tactical considerations.

DATA AND METHODS

The organizations in this study all receive funding from the Campaign for Human Development (CHD), a social action arm of the National Conference of Catholic Bishops. The guidelines determining eligibility for funding include the following requirements:

1. The project must benefit a poverty group. At least 50% of those benefiting from the project must be from the low-income community.

2. Poor people must have the dominant voice in the project. At least 50% of those who plan, implement, and make policy in each project should be persons who are poor.

3. Preference is given to groups that are innovative and demonstrate a change from traditional approaches to poverty by attacking its basic causes and effecting institutional change. CHD defines institutional change as: (a) modification of existing laws and/or policies; (b) establishment of alternative structures and/or redistribution of decision-making powers; or (c) provision of services that result in the achievement of one of the above.

4. Preference is given to projects that directly benefit a relatively large number of people rather than a few individuals (Jennings 1986).

These guidelines establish organizations as part of a social movement that works for changing the social structure and the system of reward distribution to the benefit of those in low income communities (McCarthy and Zald 1977). CHD has been funding organizations across the United States and in Puerto Rico for the past 20 years. Since its inception, CHD has given over $110 million in grants to community organizations, with over 3000 groups funded. Organizational stipends range from $1,700 to $40,000 per year, with 150 to 200 groups funded each year. While the guidelines set the parameters, the organizations are quite diverse in scope and history. Many groups have nationwide connections, such as Association for

Community Organization for Reform Now (ACORN) and various strands of the Industrial Areas Foundation (IAF), while other organizations are completely local and largely unconnected (perhaps even oblivious) to a larger social movement. The multifarious goals of the groups attest to their diversity and include rent control, job creation, worker cooperatives, and associations working against the death penalty and for tenant rights. In addition to receiving funds from CHD, these organizations all have as their goal changing their environment to the advantage of their members.

Data for this work come from a survey of all groups funded by CHD ($N = 360$) from 1987 through 1989. This sample's variation in size, scope, and location are characteristic of CHD-funded projects. Every state in the United States plus Puerto Rico had at least one group funded. I chose the groups funded by CHD from 1987 through 1989 for two reasons. First, CHD is one of the largest funders, both in terms of number of organizations funded and level of funding, of community organizations. Second, the sample by definition is comprised of poor people's organizations.

In March 1990, a questionnaire (see Appendix A) was sent to the director of each of the 360 organizations; a postcard reminder was sent to all non-respondents in May. In late July, a random sample of the non-respondent organizations was called and contact persons were asked to complete the survey. There were 191 surveys returned; however 4 of the questionnaires returned were so defective that they could not be included in the analysis. The usable response rate for the survey is 52% ($N = 187$). In addition to the survey data, interviews were conducted with 17 organizers, all of whom had responded to the questionnaire. All the interviews but one were conducted with paid staff (either the director or lead organizer of the SMO). In the other case, the past president (volunteer) joined the lead organizer for the structured interview. Informants were selected through a stratified, proportionate random sample, which was stratified by type of organization and scope. I wanted to interview both organizations that are nationally affiliated, such as Industrial Area Foundation (IAF), Association for Community Reform Now (ACORN), and Pacific Institute for Community Organization (PICO), and those that are entirely localized. It was also important to interview organizers who work in rural areas as well as those from urban groups. These data appear to be sufficient for analyzing the impact of the organizational construct on the type of collective action used.[2]

INDEPENDENT VARIABLES

The first independent variable is organizational size (*lmembr*). The number of members in the organizations in the sample ranges from 5 members to over 1000. In fact, 45 organizations have a membership of over 1000. There could be some error in this measure, as a few organizations that are community-based may count institutions as members. For instance, if an organization is made up of a consortium of churches and block clubs, a membership of seven may denote five churches and two block clubs as members although the SMO may actually represent tens or hundreds of people. Although the survey clearly asked for number of members, I suspect that in a very few cases, the membership estimate may be tainted by the confusion between individual and organizational members. Because there is such wide variance in the number of members, the log of membership is used in the analysis.

The second independent variable (*outfnd*) is the percentage of the total budget that comes from external sources. Internal funding might be derived from dues, bake sales, car washes, and advertising book campaigns. External funding consists of grants (including, but not limited to, CHD grants) and donations from organizations and individuals outside the local social movement organization. The percentage is calculated by dividing the amount of external funding by the organizational budget.

Measure of success (*meascs*) is gleaned from an open-ended survey question that asked, "How does your organization measure its success?" The responses were quite varied. A senior citizen's organization responded, "Success is measured not in winning but in the involvement by seniors." An organization that confronts immigration policies reported that "success is measured by the number of policy changes." Another group, whose members are all physically handicapped, stated "Success is measured by the number of barriers removed." Other responses included, "winning on the issues," "accomplishing our goal," "turnout," "seeing how far the members have come," "getting laws changed," "leadership development," and "when there is a reduction to the obstacles in the low-income community." After reviewing the answers, I discovered that they all fell into one of four categories: (1) publicity for the SMO; (2) having a maximum number of people involved in the issue or in the organization; (3) feeling that justice prevails or empowerment is accomplished; or (4) winning on the issue or achieving the SMO's specific goals. These four responses were then collapsed into a dichotomy. The first three (publicity, number of people involved, and justice or empowerment) were all coded 0, and the fourth (winning or achieving specific goals) was coded 1. The coding was done to differentiate between those groups that consider success to involve accomplishing specific goals and those groups that equate either participation, publicity, or the nebulous goal of justice with success.

The variable *dues* is coded by whether the organization requires the members to pay annual dues. Those organizations that require annual dues were coded 1, while those that did not were assigned a 0.

The source of decisions about group actions (*memact*) was also measured through a sequence of questions. After inquiring whether the groups engage in public actions the following question was asked concerning who chooses to do the action: "How do you decide to do a public action?" Respondents had four answers from which to choose: vote of membership, vote of officers, director decides, or other. The response indicating that members choose the actions is coded 1 and all others are coded 0.

The sixth independent variable represents interorganizational networking (*netwrk*). This variable was constructed from a question in the survey that asked, "In what ways does your group relate to similar community organizations in your area? (may circle more than one)." Nine choices were given, and the option of circling more than one was available. The nine choices included: attend each other's meetings, have joint meetings, attend areawide rallies, support other organization's public demonstrations, attend other organization's public demonstrations, lobby jointly, write joint letters, plan strategy together, and other forms of cooperation. This response item was examined to discover how many groups relate to other SMOs in multiple forms. The results range from 35 organizations that do not relate at all to other SMOs to 32 that relate in eight different ways. Because of skewness, responses were collapsed into five categories based on marginal equalization: $0 = 0$; 1 and $2 = 2$; 3 and $4 = 3$; 5 and $6 = 4$; 7 and $8 = 5$. The resulting distribution is fairly even across the five groups. This variable is important as it reflects the overall consciousness of the movement, especially for those groups that interact within a network of other organizations.

DEPENDENT VARIABLE: TYPE OF COLLECTIVE ACTION

The dependent variable in the model is collective action type (*contnd*), which is intended to differentiate between types of action used by organizations.   The *contnd* variable is measured by a scale comprised of two questions from the survey.   The first question that relates is, "How has your organization tried to achieve its goals?" There were eight possible responses to this question, including: letter writing, build coalitions, change local ordinances, lobby local funding or government agencies, public demonstrations, sit-ins, civil disobedience, and other (please specify).   The *other* category allowed a written response.   If there was no response to the first seven, then *other* was coded as either contentious (e.g., direct actions, accountability sessions) or non-contentious (e.g., house meetings) based on the response provided.   There were 14 groups that left the first seven categories blank but answered "other"; of those, six responses denoted non-contentious actions and eight indicated contentious actions.

The second question asks if anyone in the group has ever been arrested while pursuing the organization's goals.   Twenty-three groups reported that members had been arrested for civil disobedience.   A nine-point additive scale, from "letter writing" to "arrest" was developed, which demonstrates the range from non-contentious actions, such as letter writing and lobbying, to most contentious actions, such as direct action and arrest.   The scale received a reliability score of 0.66 (Cronbach alpha).[3]

The means and standard deviations for variables in the analysis are presented in Table 2.1, and the matrix of intercorrelations for all variables used in the analysis is presented in Table 2.2.   To analyze the relationships between the organizational variables described here and the style of collective action displayed by an SMO, conventional OLS multiple regression techniques were applied.   The measure of collective action (*contnd*) was regressed on the set of six measures of SMO characteristics.   Results of the regression analysis were also supplemented by material from the structured interviews.   This multiple method approach helps to foster an understanding of the process underlying the tactical decisions of the local SMOs.

The hypotheses outlined here were tested via multiple regression analysis.   Results of the regression analysis are reported in Table 2.3.

Large organizations will be more likely to use unruly tactics

Table 2.1
Means and Standard Deviations for Variables in the Analysis

Variable	Mean	S.D.*
Log of number of members (lmember)	5.58	2.23
Percentage of funding that is external (outfnd)	.63	.31
Measure of success (meascs)	.61	.49
Members choose actions (memacts)	.51	.50
Extent of relations with other organizations (netwrk)	3.31	1.43
Dues required (dues)	.80	.39
Level of contentiousness (contnd)	4.10	1.60

*Standard deviation

such as public demonstration, direct actions, acts of civil disobedience, or accountability sessions. The results indicate that the size of a social movement organization (LMEMBR) does seem to have a small, but significant, influence (B = .12) on the type of collective action taken. Usually, though certainly not always, in a poor people's social movement organization, a larger membership will allow for a greater pool of potential participants for an action (see Table 2.4).

In 1987, a large West Coast community organization invited the mayor to a meeting, and he initially accepted. After the group told the mayor they would have 1,500 people at the meeting, he laughed at them and invited them to meet with him in the 300-seat auditorium at the city hall. Organizational representatives insisted that the mayor come to their community, contending that there would be a very large crowd. Two days before the meeting, the mayor backed out. On the night of the meeting 2000 community organization members and the entire press corps arrived, but no mayor. Speeches were tightly organized at the meeting, and an empty chair with the mayor's name was prominently displayed on the platform. The press had a field day, and the mayor was publicly humiliated (White 1990).

While such an action is not as contentious as civil disobedience,

Table 2.2
Intercorrelations for Variables in the Analysis

	Lmembr	Outfnd	Meascs	Memact	Netwrk	Dues	Contnd
Log of number of members (lmembr)	1.00						
Percentage of funding that is external (outfnd)	-.23	1.00					
Measure of success (meascs)	-.12	-.12	1.00				
Members choose actions (memacts)	.11	.09	-.08	1.00			
Extent of relations with other organizations (netwrk)	.12	.04	-.07	-.03	1.00		
Dues requirement (dues)	-.03	-.04	-.01	.30	.06	1.00	
Level of contentiousness (contend)	.22	-.03	.03	.20	.47	.24	1.00

Table 2.3
Net Relationships (*B*) between Organizational
Variables and Types of Collective Actions
(*contnd*) Undertaken by Poor People's SMOs
(*N* = 187)

Organizational Variables	B	SE	T
log of number of members	.12	.05	2.24*
percentage of funding that is external	-.05	.39	.13
measure of success	.32	.24	1.32
members choose actions	.55	.24	2.21*
extent of relations with other organizations	.54	.08	6.69**
are dues required	.64	.30	2.34*
constant	.24	.59	.68
R^2	.31		
Adj R^2	.29		

** $p < .0001$.
* $p < .05$.

it does illustrate the importance of size in cases where direct confrontational tactics are used. Further qualitative evidence gleaned from the Industrial Area Foundation bulletin, *Organizing for Change*, illustrates the importance of size in direct, contentious actions. Baltimoreans United In Leadership Development (BUILD) is a group that initially was interested in correcting discriminatory lending practices in the banking industry.

Discriminatory practices in the banking industry had prevented many Baltimoreans from purchasing homes. BUILD vowed to put an end to this and to see that Baltimore residents received fair treatment.

For months, BUILD leaders had been attempting to set up a meeting with the president of one of the largest banks in the city. Leaders had frequently written and phoned him. BUILD members became incensed at his consistent refusal to meet with or recognize the organization. BUILD had taken enough.

After several strategy and training sessions, sixty leaders gathered at the bank on an appointed date. Lining up single file outside the bank, they shuddered as carloads of police with K-9 dogs on leashes came to maintain order. Armed with the fact that they all had accounts at this bank, they filed in to conduct business. The bank tellers and managers were totally unnerved as they attempted to serve their customers. Some brought in 500 pennies that they needed converted into dollars. Some wanted balances checked. Some wanted to talk about new or old accounts. Some were clumsy and dropped their change; others were forgetful and forgot their account numbers. All, however, after conducting one transaction, returned to the back of the line to wait their turn to conduct more business.   At the same time, a delegation of leaders went upstairs to the office of the president. They said they wanted an appointment, and that the BUILD members who were in line downstairs could certainly conduct business as customers all day. They had brought lunch.

Responding to the phone calls from the frenzied employees downstairs, the president offered to meet immediately. BUILD leaders replied that they had come to schedule an appointment for a meeting. He quickly gave them a date. The delegation returned to the BUILD members who were still in line downstairs and reported their victory. Much to the relief of the besieged bank employees, they all exited to the front of the building. Outside, they joyfully greeted members of the media to report the great success.

As a result of that action, early in the history of BUILD, over 250 families received mortgage loans in the city at affordable rates. The BUILD organization sent initial signals to Baltimore city power brokers that the new kid on the block was the BUILD organization and that it was there to stay! (Perry 1990, 19)

Bank actions are a favorite tool of many groups. The account of the Chicago group, whose ability to assemble hundreds of demonstrators gave even its threats clout, further illustrates the importance of size.

Two of the organizations, both of which are based in the coal-rich mountains of Kentucky and Tennessee, were becoming increasingly engaged in confrontational tactics as they grew. One organization in Tennessee was initially reluctant to "take on" the coal companies. As one former chairperson of the organization recounted:

In the beginning we were small and afraid of the owners [coal mines]. Later

Table 2.4
Net Relationships (*B*) between Organizational Variables and the Most Contentious Types of Collective Actions Undertaken by Poor People's SMOs (*N* = 109)

Organizational Variables	*B*	*SE*	*T*
Log of number of members (lmembr)	.06	.02	2.48*
Percentage of funding that is external (outfnd)	-.15	.18	.82
Measure of success (meacsc)	.13	.12	1.08
Members choose actions (memact)	.41	.12	3.48*
Extent of relations with other organizations (netwrk)	.17	.04	4.26**
Dues requirement (dues)	.22	.13	1.73
Constant	.53	.29	.06
R^2	.25		
Adj R^2	.22		

** p < .0001
* p < .01

on [4 to 6 years], as we got more members and we got madder we went to the courthouse to do a check of the property tax records and to see who owned the land. We went public with one of our findings, that one coal company owned 30% of the land in Campbell county and paid only 6% of the property tax in the county. Many of us received threatening calls after that. Later we had demos [demonstrations] and went to Nashville to make our feelings known. Later, when the Tennessee National Guard wanted to take over 20,000 acres for a new base, we really got after them—demonstrations, accountability sessions, letters to the editor of papers all over Tennessee. We beat 'em. They didn't build. (October 1991)[4]

Again, it must be emphasized that lack of size does not preclude an SMO from engaging in contentious forms of collective action; however, a larger membership seems to make it more likely that a group will engage in more confrontational or contentious collective action. Some actions do not require a large number of people, such as the action engaged in by a Dallas-based group in which three men in wheelchairs engaged in civil disobedience by using sledge hammers to make a sidewalk wheelchair accessible. However, for many confrontive actions, a large number of people is important.

As the number of members reported for some of these organizations may represent what is called "bloc" recruitment (merging several groups in a neighborhood into an umbrella organization), the impact of size on collective action may be *underestimated* in this analysis. An organization may have listed 10 members, but if it was an organization of organizations, those 10 "members" may represent hundreds of individuals. Another study may be done to analyze the differences between individual member organizations and those that result from bloc recruitment. Size of organization is also important because a larger membership increases an organization's ability to disrupt, as does its ability to command the cooperation of other organizations in its network.

It is predicted that *for poor people's SMOs, external funding will have little or no influence on tactical contentiousness.* The net relationship between external funding (OUTFND) and the style of collective action (CONTND) was small and negative, but not statistically significant. This lack of relationship directly confronts one of the critiques (McAdam 1982) of resource mobilization theory which generally asserts that if a group relies too heavily on outside funding, it will become increasingly quiescent and come to rely on less contentious forms of collective action. However, this finding indicates that the level of external funding has no measurable effect on tactical contentiousness.

As indicated, many of these organizations receive additional funding from sources other than CHD. Moreover, it would be difficult to imagine that all other funders exhibit the same propensity for change as CHD. Thus, it must be remembered that this variable is the percentage of the entire budget that is supported by external funding, and not merely the percentage of the budget that is CHD funded. Although the finding might not hold for every group under every funding source, the evidence is that poor people's social movements *may* be less susceptible to the co-optation pressure than was previously imagined.

Some analysts might suggest that because CHD expects organizations to work for concrete change and encourages innovative approaches to attacking the basic causes of poverty, organizations that receive a higher percentage of external funding from CHD may be more likely to use disruptive tactics. However, this relationship is not statistically significant ($T = -.79$; sig. $T = .43$). Furthermore, the relationship between the amount of the CHD grant and the level of contentiousness is not statistically significant ($T = .295$; sig. $T = .76$). Perhaps other external funders have similar "structural change" goals to CHD, but the data do not allow for such analysis of the goals of other funding sources. However, there may also be a more likely conclusion.

During the interviews, every community organizer was asked, "Have actions ever been influenced by how a funder might respond?" Every organizer admitted that, at one time or another in his or her career, there had been a discussion about whether there might be financial repercussions from a proposed action involving a funder withdrawing, canceling, or refusing to renew a grant. Three organizers mentioned that this discussion had centered on whether the organization would get Community Development Block Grant money if a proposed action against the city administration was carried out. Only one organizer indicated that the proposed action was tabled because of such financial considerations. Three organizers indicated that they had received "hints" not to get involved in an issue or CHD funding would be jeopardized. Two of the three went ahead with their proposed action, while one reneged on a planned contentious action based on the perceived threat.

It is possible that one might discount such fearlessness in the face of possible funding cuts as an organizer's "damn the torpedoes" attitude. However, as both the survey results and the personal interviews yield the same results, one is tempted to say that criticisms about co-optation may be invalid, at least for poor people's SMOs. The most obvious conclusion may be correct; that is, poor people's SMOs *may* be more resistant to co-optation by funding sources than previously thought (McAdam 1982; Helfgot 1974; Donovan 1973).

The hypothesis is that *poor people's SMOs which have specific criteria for measuring success will tend to use more contentious actions than those with abstract or general goals*. However, the results indicate that social movement organizations with more specific measures of success (*meascs*) are not more likely to use contentious collective action. This finding is surprising. Perhaps, some groups who have a general measure of success engage in contentious actions in confronting a specific issue. Organizations that measure success by witnessing "justice prevail" may use unruly tactics in situations of gross injustice. Connecting the measure of organizational success with the extent of success commands further attention, but for this analysis, a specific measure of success is not a predictor of contentious action.

In poor people's SMOs, if the members choose the tactics, the action is likely to be more contentious. SMOs that allow their members to choose the tactics (*memact*) do tend to display contentious collective action ($B = .55$). This relationship is statistically significant at the .05 level. It is not clear whether this proposition would fit all social movement organizations or if it is restricted to poor people's movements. These data seem to suggest that poor people do not believe in the efficacy of non-contentious forms of collective action or, at the very least, *do* believe in confrontation.

Alinsky often advised groups not to let their actions get beyond the experience of the group, advice frequently mentioned within the community organizing culture. However, this caution was directed at largely middle-class organizers leading working-class groups as in Back of the Yards in Chicago, Community Service Organizations in California, and Northwest Community Organization in Chicago. Perhaps when the poor really control the organization, it is the middle-class staff who must be willing to act contentiously. Others (Rosenthal and Schwartz 1989) have noticed a connection between direct democracy and spontaneity of action. Many of the organizations in this sample have some form of an annual convention where goals for the year are established, committee chairpersons are elected, and tactics are considered. These mass meetings and many other small gatherings where specific targets and tactics are chosen more closely resemble direct than representative democracy. An ACORN organizer in Chicago reported that the members constantly push for more innovative, and sometimes confrontational, tactics, especially as their situation deteriorates. This may stem from the limited strategic repertoires (Tilly, Tilly, and Tilly 1975) that confront poor people's organizations. The propensity of members to push for confrontational tactics may also result from a desire to use tactics that are not familiar to local elites in order to gain bargaining advantage. Most poor people who are part of formal organizations have been to countless nonproductive meetings, "danced the bureaucratic shuffle," and experienced many broken promises. Such movement organizations will not be easily assuaged but may rather choose to act contentiously. When the members are allowed to choose the tactics, there is a tendency to expand the repertoire to include more unruly tactics.

It is predicted that *those organizations that have a dues requirement will tend to engage in more contentious tactics.* Organizations that require annual dues display a greater likelihood ($B = .64, p < .05$) of contentious actions. This relationship confirms the hypothesis that the larger a stake members have in an organization, the more likely the organization is to engage in contentious collective action. It also suggests that dues do act as a "hook" on the members that induces a level of commitment and a sense of ownership in the organization. Because of the empowering aspect of dues, and because poor people have found that many other avenues of political access are closed, those organizations that require dues are much more likely to engage in unruly actions. Some of the interviewees also mentioned the importance of the "discipline" of dues (Holler 1991). This discipline, at least for poor people's organizations, seems to translate into more control by the members who, in turn, are more likely to engage in unruly tactics than if the actions are chosen solely at the discretion of an elite cadre. A further issue may be the method in which the dues are collected. Data on the method of collecting dues is incomplete; however, one federated organization claims that 45% of the annual budget for the organization is supplied by membership dues and 75% of that total is collected directly in meetings and door-to-door canvassing. For these organizations, the requirement of dues seems to facilitate emboldened tactics.

It is expected that *poor people's SMOs that meet often with similarly directed organizations will be likely to engage in more unruly tactics.* Social movement organizations that interact with, or relate to, other SMOs (*netwrk*) will be more likely to use contentious forms of collective action. This net relationship is by far the most statistically significant of any in the model ($B = .54, p < .0001$), and it demonstrates the importance of a shared identity, not only within an SMO but between SMOs, for those who engage in contentious actions.

Marx (1969) made a similar discovery when he noted that 78% of all African-Americans in Los Angeles read an African-American newspaper. He felt that this indicated the importance of a shared ideology for those who acted contentiously in the 1960s urban disturbances.

Working relationships with other organizations have social-psychological importance and are resources on which groups can draw when an action is taken. Both the shared vision and the additional people available for an action or confrontation are important. Though the question was not asked, it might be expected that relating with other groups will more often result in large demonstrations, more broad based support for an action, and a greater source of power when confronting elected officials. Those social movement organizations consisting of poor people who relate to other social movement organizations are more likely to engage in more contentious forms of action.

This finding from the survey data is also supported by the qualitative data in an interview with the director of one of the leading training schools for social movements. Located in the mountains of Tennessee, the Highlander School, which was founded by Myles Horton, has a long and rich history of education and social change. It was fertile ground for the labor movement in the 1930s and 1940s and, later, for the civil rights movement in the 1950s and 1960s. Three months prior to refusing to give up her seat on a Montgomery, Alabama, bus (December 5, 1955), Rosa Parks attended workshops at the Highlander School. The workshops centered on how to bring about the end of the Jim Crow laws of the South. These *citizenship schools*, as they were called, helped to develop the consciousness and local leadership that later became building blocks for the civil rights movement. Currently, environmental groups are using Highlander for education and for building a more broad-based movement. In 1990, Highlander hosted over 60 workshops and gatherings, involving over 2,000 people from 40 states. The current director reported that during his stay at Highlander, and probably since the beginning, groups that planned together, strategized together, and communicated with each other were far more likely to engage in contentious actions than those that tended to be more insulated from like-minded organizations. The director indicated the importance of a shared vision and observed that "groups seem to draw strength from one another." Poor people's SMOs may shift to more unruly actions when they meet together.[5]

CONCLUSION

Research on collective action can benefit from the analysis of the types of tactics used. The Midwest organization that went to the hometown of the owner of the professional football team was not performing a symbolic action; rather, the intent was to procure a political advantage. Likewise, the citizens group in the coalfields of Tennessee used tactics designed not merely to generate attention for the organization or increase membership, but rather to win concessions from the owners and managers of the coal mines. From a purely descriptive standpoint, these organizations do often use disruptive tactics such as street demonstrations, bank tie-ups, house squatting, using sledgehammers to make public sidewalks accessible for wheelchairs, confrontational accountability sessions with public officials, and actions at the residence of many of their targets. In light of the fact that many poor people's groups both form organizations *and* use disruptive tactics, Piven and Cloward's (1977) proposition concerning the efficacy of poor people's formal organizations is seriously questioned. This study, which is based solely on poor people's organizations, finds that formal organization is not an impediment to contentious action. In fact, the very structure of the organization may lead to more unruly tactics. Rather than a pessimistic view of the relationship between organization and tactics, this research indicates that organizational structure for poor people's groups may well influence tactical decisions in a more aggressive direction.

Social movement theory and research is extended by an analysis of the effects of external funding on tactics. Certainly, the funding source is an important variable to consider, yet in these organizations, which receive on the average only 31% their budget from CHD, there is still no relation between the amount of external funding and the level of contentiousness of actions. One might assume that there are other funding sources with similar structural change goals as CHD and that these organizations happen to have found them. If this is the case, it is good news for poor people's organizations that are interested in change, as funding is available from a variety of sympathetic sources. On the other hand, if CHD is somewhat unique, then this research may show the resilience of groups to co-optation. Furthermore, this research supports earlier contentions (Barnes 1987; Jenkins 1983) that organizational maturity in poor people's groups does not inevitably lead to quiescence in action. It has been found that often, the history of an organization can be a resource to be used judiciously when dealing with elites.

This research offers another way to understand the role of poor people's organizations. Outside resources can result in the empowerment of poor people's SMOs. The force of co-optation may be decreased by the organizational structure of the local poor people's organization and the goals of the elites who provide substantial resources. This work reveals that it is possible for poor people's organizations to be empowered and to resist co-optation. The result is often that public policy is challenged and changed.

The role of interorganizational networks may be underdeveloped in social movement research. Most other studies (e.g., Gillespie 1983; McCarthy and Zald 1977) have focused on the competition between organizations in the same social movement. This study finds that interorganizational relations bring solidarity and a tendency toward unruly tactics. The findings concerning the level of democracy within poor people's SMOs also have implications for further social movement research. There is considerable debate, often between students of collective and resource mobilization, concerning the supposed dichotomy between spontaneity and organization. This research supports others (e.g., Rosenthal and Schwartz 1989) who have found that direct democracy may facilitate both spontaneity and organization. Organizations that toil in relative obscurity may not be aware of the extensive network of poor people's organizations and training centers like the Highlander School and various centers staffed by IAF and ACORN personnel. Organizers might be enlightened through learning how other organizations use their history as a resource to win concessions.

A final purpose of this chapter is to examine the connection between social movement organization and collective action style. The claim made throughout this work is that there is a connection between the organizational attributes of social movement organizations and the tactical decisions an SMO makes, and specifically those of poor people's groups. Larger organizations that allow members to help make the tactical decisions, maintain a dues requirement for members, and relate often with similar organizations are the most likely to engage in contentious collective action. The influence of external funding on tactical choices, at least for poor people's organizations, is negligible. It remains to be seen if this finding and the relationship between choosing tactics and actions can be generalized to non-poor SMOs.

NOTES

1. While goals and measure of success are closely aligned, they are not synonymous. I define measure of success here as the mechanism that organizations use to discern whether goals are accomplished. Oberschall (1993) defines success as a process of attainment and Gamson (1990b) notes that part of the dimension of success involves gaining new advantages. The measure of success employed here includes estimations of what organizations intend to attain and achieve and how the SMO assesses its effects. Goals often have to do with the mission statement of an organization, whereas the measure of success addresses the issues of the manner in which an organization achieves its goals.

2. Concern about the liability of newness prompted a check of whether the older organizations in the sample were significantly different that the rest of the sample. The mean age for the organizations is not quite 11 years. A test was done on all organizations over 16 years old ($N = 33$) and it was found that they are not different from the entire sample on the items measured. I suspected that community organizations organized in the late 1960s may retain a character of contentiousness unlike the other organizations, which were founded later. According to the test of older organizations-those commencing between 1960 and 1975-there is no difference in the actions taken nor is there a significant difference in organizational structure.

Further tests of sample bias were done on the location of the non-respondents. Every state plus Puerto Rico has organizations that are funded by CHD, and in this sample, all states except Idaho, New Hampshire, and Hawaii had at least one organization that responded, including two from Puerto Rico. It appears that the Midwest and the Northeast may be a bit over-represented, but generally, the sample is representative of the geographic diversity of the CHD population. Furthermore, federated organizations are slightly overrepresented in the sample. Thirty percent of the CHD population is either a federated or national organization, while in the sample, the rate is nearly 35%. Response bias does not seem to significantly limit the findings.

3.   There may be *some* variation between poor people's organizations that receive funding from CHD and those that do not, and thus, sample bias must be addressed. It is my view that the evidence assembled here provides a reasonably representative glimpse of the most stable, grass-roots, formally organized poor empowerment groups across the United States. In addition to the scope and longevity of CHD, this contention is supported by an external review of CHD in 1988, in which a large group of unsuccessful applicants for funds was surveyed.   The reviewers found that these groups were "in most respects quite similar to the successfully funded groups" (McCarthy 1993). This study does not include a sample of organizations that were denied funding by CHD. However, because of the history of CHD, the findings of the external assessment team, and the tests done on the data for this work, it seems fair to say that the organizations funded by CHD are plausibly representative of poor people's organizations.

4.   To protect the privacy of organizers who participated in structured interviews for this research, individuals are not identified by name or organization. Statements attributed to organizers are direct quotations from interview transcripts, with no corrections in grammar or sentence structure.

5.   These findings were also tested using the only most unruly tactics (public demonstrations, civil disobedience, and arrest) as the dependent variable. Except for the dues variable, which barely misses, all other items that were significant in the nine point additive scale are statistically significant. For this subset of organizations, $N = 109$.

3

Competition: Win, Lose, or Draw

Oh dear, the Presbyterians are thinking of opening a soup kitchen. What are we going to do? —*Bea Moore*, Director, First United Methodist Church Soup Kitchen

We turn now to competition—how and why organizations compete with one another. From the vast literature of organizational theory, one can summarize the options that organizations face in relating to their environments. Organizations can compete with each other along several dimensions: they can cooperate in various ways or attack and harass one another. Although examples of each response are evident from the survey, the focus in this chapter is competition between SMOs.

We bring clarity to the issue by naming competition as an important component in our understanding of SMOs, in particular, and other nonprofit groups, in general. Dancing around the subject of competition and relegating it to the realm of organizational impoliteness is a disservice to our understanding of SMOs. We find two broad areas of competition between SMOs, with several specific categories in each. There is *territorial competition* between SMOs, which is environmental in nature, and involves turf and resources. There is also *organizational competition*, which is more structurally defined, and involves the recruitment of staff, leadership styles, definition of issues, training strategies, and recruitment of members.

Borrowing the language of biological ecology, organizational ecology theorists have much to say that illuminates competition between groups in the CHD sample. In broad terms, organizations compete when the survival of one is negatively related to the survival of another; that is, when their relationship is or approaches a zero-sum game. Organizations become freer to cooperate when both can grow in the same environment (Barnett and Amburgey 1990).

To survive, an organization must occupy a distinct niche in the environment. Hannan and Freeman (1977) demonstrate that organizations attempt to differentiate themselves from others by having a unique structure, size, or set of activities. Other researchers suggest that different approaches to ownership and governance have an impact on organizational survival and that competition may itself have direct effects on organizational structure (Rao and Neilsen 1992; Baum and Oliver 1991; Barnett 1990; Pfeffer and Leblebici 1973). If there are similar organizations competing for the same niche, the one that best fits environmental contingencies such as environmental capacity, resources, and members will survive. These contingencies tend to favor specialist organizations that can be flexible in structure. Specialists that can hold back some of their capacity have the ability to respond to environmental change, competition from other groups, and the need for action. Lean organizations that have some distinction from others in their environment and are poised to act are more likely to be survivors. Generalists—organizations that, through their diversity, have both more excess capacity and a less flexible structure—are more cumbersome.

Organizations must find their niche and understand its width. Hannan and Freeman define the fundamental niche of an organization as "the set of all environmental conditions in which the population can grow or at least sustain its numbers" (1989, 96). Organizations compete when their fundamental niches intersect. In the case of SMOs, the presence of one may affect the growth potential of another, and consequently, the groups will compete for resources, members, leaders, and turf. Consistent with the population ecology research, the SMOs in this study not only compete but attempt to define a fundamental niche that differentiates them in some way from others in both the nearby and general environment.   A stable environment favors populations of specialists. However, when the environment is variable and the fit of organizations with environmental contingencies is unclear, selection tends to favor polymorphic populations—those that contain mixtures of specialists. Hannan and Freeman (1977) propose an analogue to this when they suggest that organizations "may federate in such a way that supraorganizations consisting of heterogeneous collections of specialist organizations pool resources" (1977, 954). Turf battles between federated organizations in this study attest to this and will be discussed subsequently.

While Hannan and Freeman argue that organizations of similar size compete with each other, Barnett and Amburgey (1990) find that the presence of large organizations in an environment actually increased the viability of other organizations. Although their study focuses on early telephone companies, where mutual relationships were somewhat logical, their conclusions may help explain the entry and growth of new SMOs into areas already occupied by larger SMOs, federated groups, or polymorphic populations. Katz and Kahn (1978) offer a general model of interorganizational conflict that illuminates our understanding of the conflict dynamic, that is, what happens when organizations compete.

This look at collectives of organizations is reflected in the image of a competitive structure, which views competition as a community-level phenomenon. Brittain and Wholey (1988) see as necessary the consideration of the direct, strategic, and diffuse effects of organizational competitiveness. Staber (1992) found that populations of cooperative sector organizations not only benefit from mutualist arrangements but compete with one another in ways that detract from and diminish the benefits of a united movement. One could, in our study, see the community level as CHD funded groups, SMOs in a particular city, or SMOs in a federated group.

COMPETITION IN SMOS

Zald and McCarthy (1987a) conclude that competition between SMOs is primarily over resources and legitimacy. They offer two hypotheses that are particularly applicable to the competition for resources observed in this study: "Under conditions of the declining availability of marginal resources, direct competition and conflict between SMOs with similar goals can be expected to increase" (1987a, 164). Several organizers spoke of "problems" arising when the community or area is saturated with poor peoples' SMOs. One organizer reported knowing about 78 community groups with paid staff in a single midwestern city. Another organizer lamented, "There are different groups and models of organizing in the same city, but they are gonna draw eventually on some of the same financial resources and activists" (October, 1991).

Another Zald and McCarthy hypothesis addresses the pressure

on groups to find a specific funding niche or claim they are somehow different from other groups in the social movement industry: "The range of appeals and the variety of organizations that develop are partly related to the preexisting heterogeneity of potential supporters" (1987a, 166). One organizer summed up the issue:

When I go out and speak, they [funders] want to place us in a different pigeon hole from this group and that group, and constantly maximize the differences. They want us to present ourselves in different ways so that we can become fundable or so that we can fit their theoretical model. There's a tremendous external demand for us to distinguish ourselves from each other rather than for us to cooperate. (March 1991)

The pressure to be distinctive affects not only competition for resources but also competition for legitimacy. All the SMOs funded by CHD share the goal of social change. Groups are differentiated by the specific policies they seek to change, the level of government or institution they hope to influence, and the tactics they use. SMO leaders make statements about their group and other groups in their attempt to garner influence with decision makers and claim an impact on their local community. This competition for legitimacy—for turf, members, and media coverage—can be acrimonious. An organizer reports:

Ten years ago there was a major, major conflict between [three national groups] in a fourth of the major cities around the country. They all went to the same cities to try to organize at the same time. Huge fights. They wouldn't go into the room with each other and there were big fights. (May 1991)

Competition takes place directly when more than one group attempts to organize in the same city or area. Clearly, there are scarce resources, a limited number of activists and participants, few issues around which to galvanize an SMO, and only a limited amount of turf to be claimed. There is also indirect and more esoteric sparring, as evidenced by public and private criticism of one group by another. This type of competition is particularly evident between the major federated groups in the social movement industry.

The literature on SMOs acknowledges competition between groups but focuses primarily on the struggle for resources and a niche. As a concept, interorganizational competition seems amorphous. Competition is downplayed in much of the literature on organization

theory in favor of cooperation (Perrow 1979), several examples of
which are found in the survey data. Groups related to the Center for
Community Change coordinate goals and organizational themes. At the
Highlander School, communication and sharing information are stressed
and seem to exist among the groups and individuals trained at
Highlander. Similarly, two southern groups have annual joint
leadership retreats. An organizer for one describes the process:

For years we knew about organizations within the state and I'd always heard,
"They're just like us, but they're black." And they'd always heard, "They're
just like us, but they're white." So we decided to have a joint leadership
retreat with [them]. It helped us to understand each other and to see where our
common ground was and to see how we could work together for things. When
we go to lobby with the legislature, we can link up and support each other so
we're walking in, black and white together, and we have more power.
(October 1991)

Baum and Oliver conclude that institutional relations play a
very significant role in reducing the likelihood of organizational
mortality (1991, 213). Several institutional theorists (Oliver 1991;
DiMaggio 1988; DiMaggio and Powell 1983; Meyer and Rowan 1977)
reach the same conclusion: formal cooperative arrangements enhance
organizational survival.

Management literature tends to advocate the avoidance of
conflict except in market situations. Moreover, even in the market
there are numerous examples of interfirm coordinating structures that
limit competitive pressures. For instance, the "Baby Bells" in the
telephone system are regional, while the petroleum companies divide
the United States into regions for particular brands of gasoline.

TERRITORIAL COMPETITION

Turf

Defining turf is an important precursor to understanding why
perceived or real turf shortages lead to such intense competition
between groups. Turf is the physical area where an SMO conducts
business, recruits members, and seeks at least its initial resources. The
biological concept of niche suggests that there is a set of environmental

conditions in which a population can grow, or at least sustain its numbers. Marx, Weber, and, later, Downs pointed out the significance of the social, political, and economic conditions in which particular organizations could exist. These dimensions of a bureaucracy—or an SMO—define its niche.

A niche that will support an SMO is not necessarily unique to any one group. That is, any niche with the appropriate social, political, and economic conditions will suffice. Groups compete when a niche is available or when their fundamental niches intersect.

Perhaps the most acrimonious and emphatic difference among groups is reflected in staking out a territory, comprising the turf of the SMO. A Miami organizer ponders competition for turf by querying, "How many community organizations can one community support?" A CHD staff member reports being aware of several instances in which two or three federated organizations target the same city or region of the country. The outcome is often overt hostility:

You'd get to the point where people wouldn't go into the same room with leaders of another group. There were big fights, a lot of turf fights. It was because some of the larger groups had developed four or five major power centers and decided to expand. One group wanted to "claim" the midwest, another "claimed" northern California. (February 1991)

Another organizer suggests that competition over turf really involves power within community-organizing circles. There are as many as three concentric circles in this image: (1) individual organizers operating within (2) SMOs, which may be part of (3) a federated group. Defining the niche will become more complicated and the group will intersect with increasing numbers of more organizational niches as the circles expand.

Competition is about those connections between cities, state to state influencing policy. Clearly organizations and networks become institutions. Those become the structures within which people operate and relate and unless there's a willingness between structures to engage, to say let's work together, merge, whatever, there's going to be competition. (March 1991)

Zald and McCarthy suggest that competition over turf is related to domain and to whether domain consensus can be reached. The notion of domain consensus means that SMOs may cooperate if the "skills, competencies, tasks, and prices of the partners to the exchange are agreed upon by all parties" (1987a, 170). Organizations maintain their autonomy and may still compete in some areas even after a consensus has been reached in others. For example, a community group in Detroit that is fairly contentious established a separate housing corporation to secure properties that can be rehabilitated as low-cost housing and funds to complete the rehab. The housing corporation works within the city and public housing bureaucracies in a cooperative and solicitous manner to facilitate housing redevelopment in the neighborhood, a task the community group could not accomplish. Both groups rely on a local nonprofit legal group for counsel. Competition for external resources remains intense, but each of the three groups has specialized functions as well as a unique ground for consensus.

In the most vituperative description of turf competition, an organizer for a federated group accused two other such groups of exaggerating the number of members and the level of their involvement. Another accused a rival organizer of mobilizing a community simply as a show of force with no concomitant increase in the number of members that the SMO could claim. Other organizers reported an unwillingness to cooperate with groups because one had invaded the other's turf.

An organizer in Tennessee asserts simply, "There are turf wars." There is competition between federated groups, between intrastate groups, and between the larger groups and local community organizations. This organizer sees a loss to communities resulting from the turf struggles:

I think it's ridiculous when there are plenty of communities where there are no organizing groups for people to be competing in a turf where there are a multitude of organizations. It is a waste of resources on a national scale. In some cities, it's gang warfare, block by block while other cities have no viable organizations at all. (October 1991)

A leader of a federated group cautions his newly recruited organizers that turf struggles can be counterproductive: "I tell you guys, if I ever catch any of you on somebody else's turf, you're fired. You must respect each other. Don't sit around saying somebody is better than somebody else. You need each other. None of you is that good" (March 1991).

Resources

Competition for turf and resources is related since funds for groups flow from the geographic area in which a group is located. Obviously, since this study focuses on groups that received funds from the Campaign for Human Development, organizations do also solicit support from foundations and other financial institutions located beyond their physical boundaries. There is, therefore, competition for financial resources on the local, regional, and national levels. Even groups that organize through churches must compete with other local and denominational interests.

Continuing with the use of niche theory, Hannan and Freeman's research attempts to measure the variance of a population's resource utilization or its *niche width* (1989, 104). Whether an SMO has a discrete function or a range of functions helps determine what resources will be available. Hannan and Freeman describe the dichotomy as involving the jack-of-all-trades versus the specialist organization. The preferred niche width, that is, how generalist a group is, varies with several environmental conditions such as growth and stability.

The growth rate of the population, that is, how many SMOs can successfully occupy an area, can be understood using Hannan and Freeman's notion of carrying capacity, which measures the number of particular organizations that a society can support. The carrying capacity varies over time depending on several environmental conditions, including institutional rules, the availability of resources, and the founding, concentration, and diversity of organizations (1989, 123-144). Whether or not the carrying capacity is a moving target (as Hannan and Freeman conclude), the idea is replete with resource issues for SMOs. Institutional rules play an obvious part in the availability of funds for groups. CHD funds groups whose goals include social change; however, state and federal funding opportunities, limitations, and emphases all change with the political winds and partisan politics.

Zald and McCarthy offer a series of hypotheses about competition among SMOs, several of which focus on resources. They suggest that SMOs with similar goals will experience a greater level of conflict when resources become scarce. Heterogeneity among supporters is also important to SMOs; this allows groups to have a broader range of activities. Whether organizations are inclusive, demanding relatively little from most members, or exclusive, demanding substantial commitments, also influences the degree of competition for resources (see Zald and McCarthy 1987a).

Groups in the survey were asked to name their most important resource. Twelve named money first and 41 named it second. However, 173 groups identified people as either their first or second most important resource. The group's history of organizational success in effecting public policy was the most important resource for 8 groups, but it was the second most important resource for 100 groups. These important resources are the source of much competition. An organizer of a national group contends that organizations become more competitive as resources become more scarce. "Some are vying to be number 1, the Authentic Voice, and trying to translate that into getting grants and money" (May 1991).

There are hundreds of foundations that offer support for various community projects and groups. One long-time organizer asserts that building relationships with foundations is important. His understanding is that foundations have three criteria for awarding financial support to SMOs: training and empowerment, the ability to raise funds locally to augment foundation support, and the issues on which the group focuses. The latter causes the greatest concern for SMOs and is the reason why some groups either do not solicit foundation support or carefully target foundations that are sympathetic to particular issues or philosophies. Saul Alinsky made ignoring foundation support a cause célèbre and encouraged his followers to protect the integrity of their SMOs by seeking only community and member support.

ORGANIZATIONAL COMPETITION

Recruitment of Staff

It is clear that organizers see the recruitment of qualified staff as an activity that is crucial to the viability of the group or movement. Although organizers did not offer a unified job description for staff members, there was a pervasive sense that they seek energetic, experienced, and mature applicants. Beyond those three criteria, the qualifications varied. A staff member at CHD lamented: "Competition is going to get more intense at the local level where people are the key. A critical piece is missing: skilled organizers, skilled, experienced staff. That's the most critical piece that all of these groups struggle to find, because there are just not enough skilled organizers. Particularly minorities" (March 1991).

Representatives of two large federated SMOs defend their leadership recruitment strategies and joust over the higher ground in recruitment. One national IAF organizer contends that his groups seek careful, mature individuals with "some perspective, some maturity, some understanding of real pains and concerns that people have" (October 1991). He went on to say that, "It's really the job of the organizers to find new talent and to agitate the leaders. Having new people come in forces people to think about things differently, react, deal with new interests" (October 1991). He compares his group to groups like ACORN, which rely on younger, idealistic organizers who share a missionary zeal for their work. Certainly, appeals must be made that will attract people to movements for reasons other than compensation. This is not a bidding war. Of the 179 groups reporting an annual salary for their executive director, three-fourths paid less than $25,000 per year (in 1990 dollars). Of those, 40% paid less than $15,000 annually.

Of the two groups mentioned previously, leadership recruitment may be related to the group's philosophy. One federated group seeks to accomplish its goals by organizing actions that involve large numbers of people. It has a tendency, according to one observer, "to find people who are hot, very angry, and stir them up" (March 1991). Conversely, the other group concentrates on developing an organization that is stable and persistent; it too, engages in actions—often very contentious ones—but their mantra is to build the organization first and then act.

House (1988) argues that selecting appropriate leaders is crucial to an organization. He identifies several characteristics to be sought in leaders: the ability to perform task demands, linguistic and social influence skills, a positive predisposition to having and using power, a positive attitude, high performance standards, and an ability to convey feelings of individual empowerment to subordinates (1988, 347). No doubt, all SMOs would agree that these traits are needed for leaders, regardless of their recruitment tactics.

Leadership Styles

Saul Alinsky refered to leaders as the "gears of their own organization" (1965:46). Good leaders are essential if an organization is to function efficiently, a formula summed up by Kahn's definition of a leader as "someone who helps show us the directions we want to go and who helps us to go in those directions" (1982, 21). Nix (1976) describes the less formal leadership behavior found in most SMOs as interstitial, meaning intervening between parts. Insterstitial leaders coordinate activities within and between organizations; Nix calls their role "coordinative leadership" (1976, 315). Coordinative leaders typically have less formal authority than influence, and their influence is based on their own personality or ability and their access to scarce resources (Williams 1985, 90).

Alinsky described Haves and Havenots—individuals with legitimate, institutional power and authority and those without. Nix's typology of urban leaders offers fours types of leaders: two—the legitimizers (policy-makers) and effectors (technocrats)—resemble the Haves, while activists and the general public can be equated with the Havenots. Activists are defined as "doers and joiners at the lower levels in the hierarchy of power who have traditionally lacked technical skills and a power base" (Williams 1985, 91). The general public exerts influence by joining groups, voting, engaging in action, and influencing peers. Poor peoples' SMOs provide an example of coordinative interstitial groups, comprising coalitions of the general public and activists that can compete for resources held by the Haves in the local power structure.

Activists and the general public must increase their technical understanding of issues (why a factory must be located in a particular place, why coal mining companies profit from strip-mining, or why a sports franchise wants certain neighborhoods evacuated for a new arena) and create a power base (residents who had no recourse in the face of institutional power). Through a combination of knowledge and numbers, coordinated interstitial groups—in this case, SMOs—force change.

Much like the issue of leader recruitment, the stylistic debate is couched in the language of moral supremacy. It is not a case of winners and losers but of how the game is played. Independent SMOs typically take on the personality and leadership style of the organizer or paid executive director, while federated groups have particular organizational reputations. Groups argue, not only about whose leaders are "best," but about whose leader recruitment strategies attract the best people.

The serious debate in this category of competition is between the federated SMOs. One federated group, for example, is a church-based SMO. Organizers may be invited to assist an existing group, or they may establish a new group. In either case, the core of the SMO is comprised of church members. Their method is to take a group and its leaders and redirect its energy and power in order to effect change. The process, which is quite formal, is facilitated by elected co-chairs. An organizer describes the process by which a local group would decide to undertake an action.

To do something big, there's a process. We start with a small discussion, executive committee, lead organizer; ideas are talked through. Then it would go to a strategy team [a group of about 20] to think it through, yes or no, pluses and minuses. It takes more shape. Once that group has sorted it out, then, depending on the size of the action, it goes to a steering committee of 75 to 100 leaders to approve or disapprove the action. If it's a large action, then the delegate's congress of 400 people would consider it, lay it out, debate, approve. When COPS decides to hold an accountability session with the mayoral candidates and produce 1000 people, a group of 150 to 200 will make that decision. (May 1991)

In contrast, another group leads by knocking on doors. Organizers build chapters in neighborhoods by what one respondent described as the "bottom-up method." Although eventually, decisions are made at a convention of the membership, this group's first foray into a neighborhood tends to focus on a specific issue. The organizers pull the group together and remain in leadership positions along with indigenous leaders who emerge as the nascent chapter grows.

Definition of Issues

The way in which the SMOs in this study defined their missions and issues differs along the same lines as leadership style. Some SMOs are issue driven and, following a charismatic leader, their goal is to resolve a particular issue. Examples include tenants rights groups and environmental groups. Others develop the capacity to build power and develop leaders, a social action focus in which a disadvantaged population is organized to make demands on the larger community for justice or social change.

Groups like ACORN often mobilize a community using an Alinsky-style definition of an issue. He argued that issues must be controversial, created out of preexisting bad conditions, multiple to meet different values of the members, and specific, immediate, and realizable (Williams 1985, 120). For example, when General Motors quietly acquired property around its world headquarters building and redeveloped a residential neighborhood, dozens of low-income property owners and tenants were evicted or pushed out of their homes. ACORN, which had never been a presence in the area before, set up an office, went door-to-door to recruit members, and hastily assembled an organization of area residents who opposed the GM neighborhood restoration project. Battling GM provided a controversy. The corporation wanted to vacate a blighted area that residents saw as home, even though it was in need of rehabilitation. ACORN demanded that the project be halted or, in the event it proceeded, that the property owners be paid fair market value for their homes, that relocation expenses be paid, and that elderly residents should receive special consideration and assistance. Although the project was not stopped, ACORN was instrumental in forcing the city of Detroit to pay relocation expenses for the displaced residents and to include subsidized housing for the elderly in the completed development.

In another Detroit neighborhood, ACORN organized residents using a more nebulous target. The Michigan Avenue Community Organization (MACO) was established to prevent harm to the neighborhood. Harm is defined as any development, rezoning, plant closing, housing policy, and so on that poses a social or economic cost or threat to residents, almost all of whom are lower-income people. This group has defined enough issues to fuel an organization for nearly two decades.

In contrast to ACORN's focus on the disenfranchised, IAF groups organize through churches. Thus, IAF organizers work with a relatively homogeneous group of people who are already organized as a parish or congregation. Activity is simply redirected, and the power of the church is used to effect change. One organizer points out the strengths of this model, saying: "Good idea, good model. Resolves the resource question very nicely. Resolves the question of local leadership very nicely; you're using people who are already leaders" (May 1991). However, he suggests that the model has at least three problems. First, the church can be confining. There are some social and political issues that are off-limits for groups organized through a Catholic parish, such as advocating for abortion rights. Second, IAF organizers worry that clergy and priests benefit from the empowerment of the group. The goal of IAF is to empower members of the organization, and not simply church leaders. Finally, IAF groups tend to be homogeneous, simply because church congregations and parishes tend to be that way. The organizers mentions a particular group that may suffer because of its homogeneity.

In San Francisco there is [a group] which is church based. It has, I think, a major flaw. The most potent and active forces in San Francisco are gay and lesbian organizations and [the group] wouldn't touch those groups. [They] went after churches and labor unions. It's useful if you want to revitalize those institutions and make them players. But if you want a value base that's homogeneous, who does that leave out? It leave out people who are not in the church. (May 1991)

The Association for the Rights of Citizens (ARC) provides another example of how issues are defined and understood. ARC emerged from a group known as United Labor Unions and focuses on organizing non-traditional workers. They charge union dues at a fraction of what a trade or industrial union would charge and engage in aggressive fund-raising to provide support for the organization. ARC's functions are research, education, and training to help workers get a contract with employers. An organizer explains, "What ARC does is train people, help them in organizing, do the research on the companies, help workers find out how much profit their company makes, all those things that are important in a drive" (March 1991). In a sense, ARC is issue driven, but an organization is also being created and maintained in the process.

Training Strategies

The competition over training strategies has to do with how groups train leaders: how they enable local residents to manage and administer SMOs. Conflict here is for the higher ground, meaning the one best way to teach people how to run an organization. There are no winners or losers, but organizers certainly seem to have strong opinions about how members should be trained.

Many of the federated groups (for instance, IAF and ACORN) have training schools or institutes for local organization leaders. There are groups whose sole function is training local leadership, such as the Midwest Training Academy and Grassroots Leadership. The Development Training Institute (DTI) in Baltimore and the Pratt Institute in Brooklyn have internships in which community organizers are taught the business of community development and strategic planning. DTI trainees spend a year in the program. Four weeks are spent in classroom training in Baltimore, with the balance of the year spent in practical situations where trainers focus on teaching participants how to give an organization staying power.

An organizer of one group found that follow-up and practical experiences for trainees are crucial to the success of a training program:

People would come; they'd feel really happy at being together. They would get energized from learning the stuff, but then they would go back to their organizations where they were still fairly isolated. They'd go back and not have the on-going support to implement some of the new skills that they had gotten initial training on [*sic*]. Often they were resented by people as having gone "away" to learn. [Trainees] came back to a "who-do-you-think-you-are" attitude from members. An important lesson we learned was the need for follow-up. You can teach people a certain set of skills, but if they don't have any experience to test it on, an opportunity to reflect, it's only going to go so far in increasing that particular person's capacity and the capacity of the organization. (October 1991)

Both organizers and local leaders face difficult tasks. One staff member at CHD comments on the need for training:

The work of the organizer changed radically in recent years. When I was going to work, you needed some skills, but you could go out and knock on doors and identify people with the problem or the issue, pull them together in a house meeting and decide what you were going to do about the issue, and organize it. The work of the organizer was in building a relationship and figuring how to get into relationships with and among other people. The skilled organizers today are trainers and teachers who don't do issue work, don't do research. It is highly skilled work, a science. It's the art of being able to put relationships together. A lot of time, long hours, little money. (March 1991)

Recruitment of Members

In this category, competition is fierce and the lines are clearly drawn. Unlike the philosophical competition over issues or leadership, SMOs can indeed win the battle for members. Organizers may banter over leadership styles and the definition of issues—and these are sincere and serious debates. However, while there is no dearth of issues, there are shortages of active members, limits as to how many groups a neighborhood can support, and never enough dollars for all the promulgated needs. Organizers must offer potential members solid reasons for joining. Is the appeal to altruism—to do this for the good of the community? Would one realize some direct personal benefit from membership—for example, reducing crime or halting a private development that threatens property values? Do people have a need to belong, conform, and feel responsible?

The competition for members seems to be arranged dichotomously. SMOs may be chapter-based or based on fund-raising, homogeneous or heterogeneous, and church-based or not. Federated groups such as PICO and IAF organize through churches (often Catholic churches). They obtain permission from the local church, organize church members in the church facility, and often rely on an already established indigenous leadership. Members who participate in the activities of an SMO under the church's umbrella are not likely to have the time and energy for organizers who recruit door to door or use an issue to generate interest. One organizer sees the church as a base from which to expand the group. "If I've done my job, those church people will reach out to the unchurched people. We can have churches, civic clubs, block clubs. Diversity is good" (May 1991). This approach to organizing seems to be an effective way to compete for members. The church lends legitimacy, and the group expands both within and beyond the church.

Organizers in a western state describe competition between two federated groups: "When you're talking to the same people, people have to make choices. With institutional based organizations, I'm not sure it makes sense to have two in the same area because they compete with each other rather than serve folks well" (February 1991). Speaking about competition between these groups, an organizer for one of them describes a dichotomy in recruitment:

[They] had a regional approach. So everybody that was interested in building a regional organization liked that. The way [we] talked was more out of a local church, congregational perspective. It's primary organization was the local church, local leaders. It was the top-down versus the bottom up approach. I think in a lot of ways many of the movement things are top down. It's folks identifying cutting issues and mobilizing people. In civil rights, they went out and interviewed people and asked what they would like to see happen. They publicly gathered folks to a cause. Not that it's disconnected from what people feel, but whether structures are put together intentionally. People aren't pulled by the nose. But it's different when the pastor says the bus is parked outside and here's what we'd like you to do. (May 1991)

Alinsky-style groups seek members by canvassing a neighborhood. Armed with anger and an issue, organizers go door to door in lower-income neighborhoods to recruit members. One midwestern organizer describes the competition between an Alinsky-style group and a federated group:

I don't think [the Alinsky-style group] ever opposes anybody coming into anywhere. [They] will go anywhere they want, not ask any questions, and do what they want. The more the merrier. If there can be three groups kicking up shit, it's better than one of us. [They] would not lose any sleep over [us] coming into a town where they were for two reasons. One, they just don't care. Two, the ways in which the organizations are built are totally different. You can have a church group with members in one of our projects and [the Alinsky-style group's] door-knocked members. (February 1991)

The organizer went on to say that while the first group does not mind the competition, his group would rather not compete with other groups for members.

There is a debate about whether a homogeneous group is easier to organize. In the interviews, many organizers suggested that groups of similar race, ethnicity, or income tend to gel more quickly. Most claimed that their group was heterogeneous and wanted to accuse some other group of looking alike. In one southwestern city there are two major SMOs, one that is Mexican and Catholic and one that blends Hispanic, Anglo, and African-American members. Interestingly, organizers of the former were instrumental in establishing the second group in order to encourage diversity. Since all the groups in this study have poor people as their members, the groups are similar across income categories. However, one national group lays claim to representing and organizing in the poorest and most disenfranchised neighborhoods.   Organizers of the rural poor report both less competition for members and generally homogeneous groups.

CONCLUSION

Whatever the point of the competition—whether income, race, or neighborhood boundary—almost without exception, organizers said they would rather not have another SMO in their vicinity competing for members. Some were more adamant than others about wanting to stake out a territory within which they could find members.   Several organizers reported occasions when vociferous objections were made to the appearance of other groups.   Without a doubt, there is competition between groups for members, and it is not amicable.

We find much evidence of competition between groups. Interorganizational frays condense into two broad categories, territorial and organizational. *Territorial competition* is more straightforward because there can be clear winners and losers. One group wins a grant from a local bank, while the other groups do not. Groups in this study received funds from CHD, while others were denied. As concerns turf, one SMO may organize a neighborhood and justify its existence to residents while another group in the area may flounder. A federated group may claim a section of Detroit and fend off other groups that want to recruit in the same area.

Organizational competition—involving struggles over staff, leadership styles, issues, training strategies, and members—is equally acrimonious. However, there is a philosophical bent to this category of competition. Groups want moral victory in these components. They want not only staff, but the best staff and the best recruitment methods, and not simply issues, but the clearest and most democratic processes of defining issues. The debates are fierce, even though the substance is often a nebulous concept.

4

Understanding the Lay of the Land

Shit, they hold up everybody's block grant contract. I don't think they're competent enough to use it as a tool. —An Organizer

As a result of the increasing emphasis placed on environmental factors, collective action research, like social movement studies, has moved from an individual focus to include both political opportunities and expected ramifications of actions and tactics. Other writers have used political opportunity (McAdam 1982), social dislocation (Piven and Cloward 1977), or external polity (Knoke 1990) to describe the milieu of movement organizations. This analysis centers on the more micro-level issues concerning organizational relationships with local officeholders and the system of local elections. It does not focus on the outcome of the action but does demonstrate that actions change depending on who is in office, the structure of local elections, and the national political mood.

Since 1975, many students of collective action (Olzak 1989; Tarrow 1988; McAdam 1982; Tilly 1978; Tilly, Tilly, and Tilly 1975) have used event history analysis to study changes in collective action over time. Others (Pizzorno 1978; Tilly, Tilly, and Tilly 1975) have used the same method in an attempt to discover cycles of protest. This approach (Olzak 1989), which often uses archival records, newspaper accounts, organizational histories, and organizational newsletters, expands the scope of collective action from individual rationality to include political opportunities. Political opportunities may include regime changes and shifts (Tilly, Tilly, and Tilly 1975), analysis of the relative strength or weakness of states (Birnbaum 1988), changes in population (Piven and Cloward 1977), and changes in voting patterns

(McAdam 1982; Piven and Cloward 1977).

Many of the earliest writings that connect political climate to the style of collective action come from political science. Lipsky (1968) wrote that groups use protest as a political tool, and consequently must appeal to the organization itself as well as to the media, third parties, and those who can grant the goals. Eisinger (1973) notes the importance of the style of government in a given city and the relation of style to the type and level of protest. Others (Spilerman 1976; Stark, Raine, Burbeck, and Davison 1974) mentioned the characteristics of cities and analyzed whether they affected the probability of an urban riot. More recently, researchers (Tarrow 1988; Tilly 1985) have included state formation, the openness of the political system, and media response as political climate variables that help to shape the type of action used. Other approaches to community action have considered displaced material and political interests (Castells 1977; 1978). Some have noted the potential for political cleavage within neighborhoods (Wylie 1989; Agnew 1978; Perin 1977), while others (Hall and McIntyre Hall 1993; McIntyre Hall and Hall 1993; Davis 1991) have attempted to examine the impact of property interests on community actions.

Political climate includes the structure of the local government (e.g., strong mayor-weak council, weak mayor and council, or city manager) as well as whether council members or alderpersons are elected in district, at-large, or nonpartisan elections. For our purposes, political climate also refers to the relation of the local community organization with the highest-ranking elected or appointed official. Usually, the mayor is the highest-ranking official, but occasionally he or she will be a member of city council, or sometimes, the city manager. A real or perceived ally, as opposed to a political official who is not beholden to the organization, will result in differing forms of collective action. Finally, political climate refers as well to the change in national policies and national administrations in the last 20 years.

The primary data source for this chapter is comprised of structured interviews with 17 community organizers. These organizers represent diversity in geography, scope, size, and focus in poor people's organizations. (See Appendix B for the list of questions asked and Appendix C for a list of organizers interviewed.) Others (Tarrow 1988) have noted the shortcomings of survey research as it relates to how behavior (collective action) interacts with other groups, opponents, and the state. This analysis combines interviews with the national survey and includes a brief overview of the political history of a few of the cities involved.

The cities range in size from Chicago's 8 million inhabitants to Miami's 358,000. All have substantial minority populations, although Chicago remains the most residentially segregated large city in the United States. Miami has the most modern form of government, while Detroit and Chicago still have vestiges of the political machine. Often, the cities in the South and West have city managers while northern cities have strong mayors. These generalizations hold true in this sample of eight cities.

CHICAGO

Harold Washington was the first black mayor elected in Chicago's history. He was a state legislator in Illinois from 1965 through 1977, and served one term in the House of Representatives (1980 through 1982) before focusing on a local race. Starks and Preston (1990) indicate there were at least three critical events that led to Washington's ascent. First, there were redistricting proposals at the city, state, and federal levels, which led to intense organizing by black community leaders and eventual victory on all three levels. There was also a massive voter registration drive in 1982 that added more than 100,000 voters, almost all of them potential Washington supporters. The crumbling of the infamous political machine continued as Michael Bilandic, and then Jayne Byrne, succeeded Richard J. Daley. While mayor, Byrne and Richard M. Daley (the current mayor) engaged in heated public battles over the remnants of the machine, and as a result, the already shaky machine was further weakened. Many community organizers supported Washington's candidacy and worked for his election (Gills 1991), giving rise to high expectations and facilitating the understanding of Washington as an outsider and a reformer. Chicago has partisan district elections for its 50 alderpeople. (See Clavel and Wiewel [1991] and Browning, Marshall and Tabb [1990] for a more complete recent political history of the city.)

SAN ANTONIO

San Antonio is the only large city in the United States in which Americans of Mexican descent are the majority. When San Antonio was founded in 1718, 70% of the population was of Mexican origin (Brischetto and de la Garzaand 1985), and when Henry Cisneros was elected mayor (1981), 54% of the population was of Mexican origin; at that time, the African-American population was 8% (Munoz and Henry 1990).

Like Chicago, San Antonio had been controlled by a political machine for many years. The last of these machines, the Good Government League (GGL), controlled city politics from 1950 to 1977. This machine was controlled by Anglos and was primarily focused on maintaining the privileged position of the whites and their neighborhood, which was located to the immediate north of the downtown area. In 1977, the electoral process was changed from an at-large system of electing council members to a single member district system. Councils since 1940 had often included token Mexican-Americans on the 10 member council, but by 1981 the council had 5 white members and 5 minority members (Munoz and Henry 1990).

Cisneros, at age 33, was the first Mexican-American to be elected mayor in 140 years and also one of the youngest in San Antonio history. He was first elected to the council in 1975. While he was initially linked to the GGL (Munoz and Henry 1990), Cisneros later dropped his affiliation and became a partner with some of the community organizations. Cisneros was mayor until 1989. (See Miller and Sanders [1990]; and Johnson, Booth, and Harris [1983] for further detail on the politics of San Antonio.)

DETROIT

Coleman Young was elected mayor of Detroit in 1973 and held that office for 20 years. Young's radical past included fighting with his foreman at a Ford factory and union organizing in both the AFL-CIO and the National Negro Labor Council. Young was also "invited" to testify before the House Committee on Un-American Activity. He was elected mayor based on promises to fire the police commissioner and attract businesses downtown. In his 1973 campaign literature, he pledged: "I will lead a business resurgence that will produce jobs by the thousands, revitalize downtown, and rejuvenate the entire city. I will move Detroit forward on a program that includes new port facilities, a stadium, rapid transit, recreational facilities, and housing."

By the time Young ran for re-election in 1977, he had become a national political broker, due in part to his early endorsement of Jimmy Carter for president. Young's close relationship with Carter resulted in Young's appointees landing jobs in the Carter administration and also facilitated a continual flow of federal money for downtown development projects. These projects included the Renaissance Center, which is a shopping, business, and restaurant high-rise on the Detroit River; Joe Louis arena; Riverfront West Apartment complex; and the Millender Center, an apartment and office tower. However, by the 1980s, Detroit was in serious economic trouble. Unemployment was 15% (black unemployment was 25%); Parke Davis, a leading pharmaceutical plant in the city, closed, idling 2,000, and Uniroyal closed meaning that another 5,000 jobs were lost. From 1979 to 1980, Wayne County, which encompasses Detroit and other municipalities, lost 100,000 manufacturing jobs (Jones and Bachelor 1986). The downtown anchor, Hudson's city block department store, closed in 1982. The priority of Mayor Young continued to be downtown development, and this emphasis increased the neglect of the neighborhoods.

The 9 city council members all run at-large in a nonpartisan election every four years. While Detroit does have a mayor-council form of government, there is unanimous agreement that the power resides almost exclusively in the mayoral side of the equation. (For a political review of the Young administration see Darden, Hill, Thomas and Thomas [1987]; Jones and Bachelor [1986]; Georgakas and Surkin [1975].)

MIAMI

Miami's political scene is inextricably linked to the Dade County environment, perhaps more so than any other major metropolis that has a countywide government system. Warren, Corbett, and Stack (1990) report that the metropolitan form of government established in Miami-Dade County in 1957 was the first of its kind in the country. There are two entities in this government structure: the county, which includes a large unincorporated section, and the cities of Dade County (including Miami and 25 other municipalities). The municipalities maintain their own police and fire departments and set their own taxes, while the county-wide Metro commission has authority over mass transit, public health, and parks.

The county-wide piece of this political pie has a commission-mayor-manager form of government. The 8 commissioners and mayor are elected in county-wide at-large, nonpartisan elections. Miami's city structure is similar with a 5 member council including the mayor, who has few distinguishable powers beyond those of other council members. As with the Metro government, there is a city manager who has administrative power and is hired by the council.

Until the 1960s, Anglos controlled both the Metro council and the council-manager offices in Miami. Now, however, the Miami council is controlled by Hispanics and African-Americans, while the Metro offices are yet dominated by whites. Other observers (e.g., Mohl 1988) have noted three important aspects of the political climate in Miami: (1) the tri-ethnic nature of the population encourages ethnic block voting; (2) because there is a high degree of residential segregation, there are intense battles over territorial issues (e.g., zoning and location of public housing); and (3) the two-tiered government structure, which is dominated by at-large elections, stifles some of the smaller cities and county-wide interests. (See Warren, Corbett and Stack [1990] and Miller and Pozzetta [1988] for more information.)

OAKLAND

While Berkeley has long been associated with radical politics and San Francisco is often viewed as the most beautiful and most cosmopolitan of all U.S. cities, neighboring Oakland has been primarily known for sports teams and the Black Panthers. Until Lionel Wilson's tenure as mayor began in 1977, Oakland maintained a political system that featured a weak mayor, a strong city manager, and at-large elections. Browning, Marshall, and Tabb report that, "Behind the formally nonpartisan politics of Oakland stood a powerful combination of corporate interests, Republican party leadership, and control over the local media" (1990, 63). Part of Wilson's agenda was to change the structure of politics in Oakland. He gathered momentum for a change from at-large to district elections, and as a result, minority representation rose to over half the nine member council by 1981. Wilson also advocated a reduction in the powers of the city manager.

(See Browning, Marshall, and Tabb [1990] for a more complete history of Oakland's political pilgrimage.)

STRUCTURE OF LOCAL ELECTIONS

The debate concerning at-large council districts began shortly after the civil rights movement began to cool. Many community organizers claimed that at-large elections allowed past injustices to continue because minority neighborhoods could not form coalitions to get representation. The fact that some cities (San Antonio, Oakland, and Miami) had included "token" minorities in elected positions did not appease the under-represented neighborhoods. By the early 1970s, the players in the local political game had begun to change. The population of most large cities was increasingly dominated by people of color, which led to increased pressure for district council elections. Oakland, San Francisco, and San Antonio all moved from at-large elections to district contests. Generally, community organizers helped lead the fight for district elections, and most considered the shift in the political climate to be progress for people of color and the poor. However, some organizers pointed out that district elections have not been the panacea that many had hoped. Among others, Gary Delgado, who has been organizing for 20 years in numerous cities throughout the country makes this observation:

That battle has been waged all over the place. Is there proportional representation? People of color fight that battle in many towns. The equation then becomes representation equals power, and that isn't necessarily true. It's a trick bag. Representation doesn't necessarily equal representation. There's a lull while people figure that out. For instance, Elliot Harris ran as the second black candidate in Oakland. The first black candidate, it is generally understood, didn't act in the interest of black people; he was in the pocket of development and his constituency is very clear. His major money doesn't come from the black community. (May 1991)

Others noted that there were organizing "problems" that came from a strong campaign for district-level elections. One individual explains:

The kinds of actions, the degree of tension, the degree of combativeness is going to be dependent on a couple factors. One is the state of need; people with greater needs take more risks. Two is the level of experience with elected leaders. There is a reluctance to move strongly on someone you helped get elected. In Oakland we fought for district elections and elected a minority city council and mayor. There was a sense that if we did that, things would be better. Not necessarily true. In the last election, minority black incumbents got beaten badly. People began to see through the color issue and see that they were not being responsive to their constituents. It takes two or three years for a new politician to claim or disclaim his constituency. Now they sit on them in the first year; accountability is much more direct and immediate. (May 1991)

One organizer in Miami took the minority view that at-large elections are an aid in community organizing. (It should be remembered that neither the city of Miami nor the county-wide government have district-level elections.)

I think it's good to have several targets. If it narrows down, it becomes a more charitable response—the one powerful person gives you charity. Dade County voters will be asked to district the county instead of electing nine at large. There a people who feel disaffected, blacks, Hispanics. My position as a professional organizer is that is not going to be helpful, to district. What is does is parochialize how you can gain the attention decision makers. It limits your access. Presently, all of the commissioners have to be leery—they don't know if we can swing some issue. (August 1991)

This organizer was the only one of 17 organizers interviewed who indicated that at-large elections could be useful in community organizing.

The situation in Detroit is different. Nine council members are elected at large, and the mayor is extremely powerful. Organizers there mentioned the control that the mayor has on the city.

The strong mayor and weak council has a serious effect on the types of actions that a community organization can and will do. The council is owned by the mayor, therefore there are no checks and balances, therefore the mayor has pretty much had carte blanche to punish community groups that are too vocal. The council members are not beholden to any particular community organization and they keep getting re-elected. Why should they be worried if they know they are going to be re-elected? And that is the part that I believe we as citizens have to be held responsible for. Our own unwillingness to get out and vote and to be politically active. And so, consequently, the major community organizations in this town who might otherwise protest constantly have to ask themselves what is it going to cost. (May 1991)

Others in Detroit, including the chairperson of the board of an organization widely thought to have been punished by Mayor Young, disagreed. He and his organization regarded the loss of city funds as business-as-usual, rather than a penalty for taking actions that embarrassed the city. When asked if recent cuts in the group's block grant were seen as punishment for taking on the mayor, the organizer responded:

No, I don't think so. I think the Mayor saw that he could do it and he had the votes on Council, so he did it to everybody. It wasn't just us. The only time we have been singled out is with building inspectors. I think we get singled out when the building inspector comes around and does one of our houses that they're remodeling, because I think there's some innate anger with CEDD [Community and Economic Development Department] and with the Building and Safety Engineering over our fights on abandoned housing. Shit, they hold up everybody's block grant contract. I don't think they're competent enough to use it as a tool. I think the city is just totally incompetent in the way they put out contracts, and they couldn't punish you any more with business as usual. I mean, when it takes you two years to get a contract anyway, how could they punish you? I mean we just got their contract signed and we're one of the first ones in the city to get it signed for last July. We had a $150,000 contract and they already owed us $90,000 for expenditures for administration. We just got our last check to bring us up to date, and it was $90,000 total. I mean you can't get any worse than that. So no, they're not smart enough to punish us. The point I was making is that the city is our largest source of money and we never would consider that in hitting the city on an issue. (April 1991)

Chicago has a strong mayor and district election of alderpersons. While Richard J. Daley was in office, community organizations often worked through the precinct captain or alderperson, but with the end of the older Daley regime came an erosion of the patronage network. When Harold Washington first came to office, he encouraged community groups to work through him. One community organizer in Chicago described the process:

The alderperson system is kind of a problem. Chicago is a problem because people for years had under the old Mayor Daley a very strong organization with a strong precinct captain and a strong committeeman and alderman. If you wanted to get something done, you went through the regular organization. That sense of how you get things done has continued with people despite the breakdown in that system. The aldermen are nothing anymore and have no ability to accomplish anything. They're basically powerless except when it comes to legislation and then there are 50 of them that you have to move, 26 to win. It's a hugely different experience from cities where people are not used to having a city council person accountable to them. Basically, here it's been our experience that we need to move people away from their dependence on the alderman and precinct captain which is sort of possible because there is no longer a precinct captain anyway. We've found in black neighborhoods it's very rare. The organization when Harold got in fell apart, and Harold set up a system of "you come directly to me to get things done: to me and my departments." You don't go through your alderman because he didn't have the majority on the City Council. So he wanted to set up his structures outside of the aldermen where citizens could relate to him to get things done. And the problem being that the old folklore in the communities is still that you work though your regular organization or your political organization. And so what we find is constantly needing to move people away from going to their alderman and going directly to someone who can get the job done. (February 1991)

While the discussion usually focuses only on urban forms of government, visits to Tennessee and Kentucky raised an issue concerning the situation of rural polity. One of the organizers pointed out that in Kentucky, there are 120 counties, each with its own government. Because many of these counties are quite poor and small, the lack of funds for schools and environmental cleanup are often key issues. Thus, when groups organize against toxic dumping or strip mining abuses, the local polity reports (often quite truthfully) there is no money for such efforts. While conducting interviews in the region in the early autumn of 1991, several counties were reporting that they would discontinue the use of school buses because of lack of funds. Organizers said that this occurs nearly every year in some counties and that children must be eithr driven to school or walk to school or else drop out until the following year, when the buses run again.

Some groups have organized and pushed through a mineral tax that forces the coal companies to pay taxes based on the unmined resources, namely coal still in the ground. This mineral tax will have substantial benefit for the local governments, as 66% will stay in the individual counties. In spite of this legislative victory, all organizers reported that the small-county system of government, combined with the area's precarious financial condition, tends to lead to less contentious forms of actions at the local level. Such a system also leads to a confusion about who is to blame for failing to have toxic waste removed, and locating a specific local target is often important for effective community organizing. Certainly, the form of government in rural areas, combined with the weak financial status, may lead to quiescence in action at the local level.

RACE AND ETHNICITY

Virtually every major American city has had a mayor of color in the past 20 years. Often, the councils or commissions in these cities are dominated by people of color. It has been noted (Starks and Preston 1990; Walton, 1985) that political behavior by African-Americans often involves a variety of political patterns, experiences, and activities. "Black political behavior is not ethnic political behavior. Despite the similarities, it is different" (Walton 1985, 8). Walton argues that reseaarchers who study black political participants and politics must be cognizant of how the structural and contextual variables constrain and limit political behavior. Many community organizations have been confronted with a mayor or a majority of council members who are people of color. In some cities, this has changed the nature of organizing.

When an organization has a personal ally in a position of authority, it is often thought that the actions of the group will become more quiescent—even if conditions fail to improve or even deteriorate further. This is believed to be especially true when the ally and the community organization are from the same racial and ethnic group. Such a hypothesis only seems logical, but in fact, the outcome depends on perception. The perceived ally may not be an ally at all, and the constituency of a community organization may not receive more benefits, and indeed, may receive fewer. Because of structural constraints, personality clashes, or differing political agendas, a mayor of color may not demonstrate an affinity toward communities that are of similar ethnic or racial background. Nonetheless, the perception of an ally in high places may induce quiescence among the members of an organization, at times regardless of the organizational construct or other factors that constitute the political climate. One community organizer, who has been in the field for more than 20 years, indicates that the trend toward quiescence has begun to turn and organizations are demanding accountability from the mayor, even if he or she is a perceived ally:

I think the other thing particularly in the inner cities which had a major impact on the number raised is the increase in minority mayors, city council members. Where it was you could often organize a community around racial questions. It was the "white power structure" making all the decisions. Most of the major cities have Black or Hispanic mayors, those who are good politically, upon whom to build a political power base to become very effective in buying off neighborhood activists, encircling them, bringing them in to look at what they did, cutting deals with the neighborhood activists. Making them feel that they've got their guy in their power. All they have to do is call up the mayor and he'll produce. It's very difficult to organize a black neighborhood with a black mayor. It's becoming easier because they're beginning to recognize it doesn't matter what color the mayor is, he or she's the mayor. (May 1991)

Often, however, it is a racial or ethnic connection that restrains normally contentious collective action. An ACORN organizer in Chicago recounted that many actions that the group undertook while Byrne or Sawyer were mayors—such as house squatting, demonstrations at City Hall, and traffic tie-ups—were not performed when Harold Washington was mayor. She emphasized that this was not because conditions were different but because ACORN members felt that, "Harold was our man, one of us, and we [didn't] want to embarrass him." Sometimes an action may not be halted but rather shifted so that a perceived ally is not implicated. The action undertaken against the owner of the professional football team in Chicago was done at the home of the owner mostly because of the greater media appeal, but also so as not "to embarrass the mayor [Washington]":

Harold was a good guy and we found a way to work with him, but we couldn't do actions on him. There's no way we could do actions so we had to sit tight for years. Nobody wanted to do an action on Harold and neither did we. It was an exciting moment in Chicago history. We walked in the same time Harold did, accidently. So, the first black mayor who is new—you're stuck with that situation. You really can't raise a ruckus. That was very difficult from an organizing standpoint. What we did over time was we developed a system of working with the administration where we would let them know we were doing actions on their department when and where so that they could be prepared to respond in some kind of reasonable fashion. We only developed that, though, close to his re-election in 1987, so in late '86 is when we developed that system. So we just had to sort of sit through the rest. We did little actions or big actions on little officials, but you could never wind up in the mayor's office. What we ended up doing is developing an ability to do big actions on department heads and let them know that we were coming. And if they wouldn't budge, they knew we were coming, but let everybody in the administration know that they weren't gonna budge we were gonna come down and make their lives miserable. It was a bureaucracy. They had a hard time moving fast enough to stop us from hitting, but they could at least get organized to be prepared to respond appropriately. Harold was never seen as the enemy, it was always a department head or the bureaucracy. So we supported Harold for his re-election based on the commitments of the guy who ran the housing campaign. But everyone knew, including the people we were negotiating with that we had no ability not to support him. That's a difficult position to be in. (February 1991)

Another community organizer in Chicago recalled a similar phenomenon. This community organization, which is located just west of the "Loop," is dominated by African-Americans.

When Washington was in the dynamics were that you have a black organization and a black mayor and the black community as a whole did not want to create something real negative for the mayor. At large, people are saying, our guy is in, let's try to work with him. Let's be on the same team. The problem is the people whose homes are being taken[,] whose neighborhood was here, were saying, "It's not to our benefit to sit back and let what happened happen, because we're gettin' screwed." We had small meetings with the mayor where he said, "What do you want?" He met personally, on several occasions, with people from this organization. We said we don't want a stadium, but that wasn't what he wanted to hear. Then what he tried to do was come into the community and meet with people in the area, set up small meetings. But because of our network, anytime something like that happens, we know about it. So he came to somebody's home, 50 people were there. They said, "Look, you've got to rethink this thing." There was no press. It was like community in community. With Washington the pastors were very hesitant to do any type of public action. They were. And it also depends on where the churches were in relation to the project. If a Bear's [football] stadium were to be built and 75,000 people would come to a game on a Sunday afternoon with tailgate parties before, any [churches] within [a certain] mile radius were saying: "No matter what, this is gonna hurt us. It's gonna hurt our Sunday service, our interests." The further you got away from this immediate area, the more likely they were to say to us, "Look, you guys aren't on the right track." With Daley [the current mayor, there is] no controversy. With him being white and constituency being more white, he dealt with the black community differently. While Washington wouldn't be attacked by the black community, the black community would attack Daley. So Daley wouldn't want to give them a reason—he was more of a negotiator. People were afraid he'd be one way for the first couple years, and then do what he wanted. But we feel we're in a good position. (February 1991)

Coleman Young was elected mayor of Detroit in 1973, but organizers there report that "only within the last five years [of his tenure] have our members been willing to oppose the mayor" (May 1991). One organizer, who formerly worked in Detroit, reported: "The group I worked with did not have any trouble embarrassing Coleman Young, but then most of the people in the organization hated him. But I know lots of other organizations who would not join us, even though they agreed, because they did not want to embarrass Coleman Young" (May 1991). An African-American organizer in Oakland and Berkeley who has been "in the business" for many years compared the situation in Detroit, where the mayor leads a city that is 70% black, with the situation in Berkeley:

Well, Coleman is the biggest sin in America. But it's different. Blacks are only 20% in Berkeley. So you have a real minority mayor. There were some people of color who had no compunction about jamming him; Latinos didn't. There was a coalition of people, some of them black, who didn't like Gus. They would go after him politically in a variety of ways. They didn't have an organized base to bring out hundreds of people. But they'd embarrass him at City Council, leak things to the press. (May 1991)

When Henry Cisneros was elected mayor of San Antonio in 1981, one of the local community organizations that had been vigorously pressing for city services on the west side ceased to engage in direct confrontation. This is partly "because services were better [e.g., drainage, sidewalks] but partly because we did not want to publicly damage the mayor" (May 1991). The current lead organizer of Citizens Organized for Public Service (COPS), which is almost exclusively a Hispanic organization, spoke of the racial ethnic dynamic in San Antonio concerning the proposed construction of a downtown sports arena. He also reflected on his tenure as an organizer of a "white" organization in Detroit:

Well, the dynamic existed [cautious tactics when a racial and/or ethnic ally is in office]. That's true with any minority group. When their people are in power, you're pulling apart people's guts. A case in point is the dome project—to go toe to toe with Cisneros publicly, knowing that he was going to be measured at the ballot box. It's one thing to oppose Henry Cisneros on an issue where the council has voted—and we've won some and lost some of those. But to do it where you're gonna measure at the ballot box was a hell of a risk. And one that was not taken lightly. That stuff was sorted through because obviously Cisneros' credibility in the Hispanic community is very hot and so is COPS.' And it really kind of tore people apart. Voter turnout was off in that election, we think in part because people just didn't want to choose. They were confused and they didn't want to deal with it. Now, the fact that exists and whether or not and how an organization deals with it are two different questions, I think. It's a universal and you're always gonna have it. (May 1991)

When asked if he felt the situation was similar in Detroit when Coleman Young was mayor, the organizer commented:

It's hard to compare. Sure it existed. I don't think it's peculiar to a particular political situation. But it's a different arena because you don't have the same level of power. My experience in MACO [Michigan Avenue Community Organization] was very different because MACO wasn't powerful in the black community. There were African-Americans involved, but that wasn't the base. The base was the white Polish community, and they hated his [Young's] guts. (May 1991)

The goal here is not to publish case studies about the political scene of each of the cities, as the politics of each are distinct, as are the community organizations. However, the tentative pattern suggests that the identity of the officeholder does make a difference in the types of actions used by social movement organizations, regardless of the organization's general proclivity.

A former ACORN organizer who now works with the Center for Third World Organizing mentioned that sometimes it depends on the community group's perception of the power that an official wields rather than ethnic and racial considerations:

The mayor of Oakland, a really strong target. I wouldn't put any of my people up against him, especially black people. He'll play this "I'm just a new black mayor," and beat them like a drum if they have no experience. That would just set people up to get screwed. Obviously when Gus Newport was mayor of Berkeley there were lots of possibilities for groups, especially black groups. He was black, progressive. Initially that might have been true that we [black organizations] did not want to do actions against him. But as things progressed we changed. When Gus fucked up, Gus got jammed. (May 1991)

NATIONAL AND INTERNATIONAL CLIMATE

Some organizers insisted that is less controversial organizing occurs nowadays than in the 1960s. They mentioned the retrenchment of many of the young people and a trend toward a more individualized outlook on life. Many organizers spoke almost longingly for the "good old days" of the civil rights movement, the womens movement, or the anti-war movement. Seemingly simultaneous with this call to the past is a belief among many organizers that today's organizations are stronger and that their tactics result in more concrete gains. A person who has organized on both coasts and acted as a consultant to numerous groups captured the sense of change in mood and tactics:

Twenty years ago people didn't say "What do I make?" People said, "Ah, this exciting, how can I help?" Now they want to know, "What do I make, what are the vacations, what do I start out at, what are the pensions?" I just think it's tied to the mood of the times. I do think there was a change in the' 80s under Reagan with his emphasis of decontrol, deregulation, bringing the country back to be proud. "We can do whatever we want, etc." The rich did get richer and the poor did get poorer and that's just a reality. The mood that it gave towards people is that that's where the emphasis should be: make as much money as possible. I think that came from Reagan. There's a backlash to a lot of the stuff that happened in the 1960s and 1970s. People think it's not effective, that you gotta work harder, that's the way you're gonna get ahead. There's a much more reactionary mood than there was back then. (February 1991)

There has been a good deal of discussion concerning the effect of the national political scene on community organizing. In the interviews with organizers, their responses included social-psychological issues, a retreat or retrenchment posture in community organizing, involvement in elections, and a rethinking of some of the tactics. This section will explore these issues as they relate to how the national, and sometimes the international, political climate influences the type and style of actions engaged in by a community organization.

Not all community organizers were pessimistic about the mood of their constituents, and many saw the Reagan-Bush years as a tool to motivate people to act. Many who had been dubious of the efficacy of electoral politics on the national level indicated that they had changed and now felt that local communities should be involved in national elections:

We focus on national politics because we think that that's the key to changing the country. And that people tend to focus on the presidential elections every four years as the one time when they focus on the national issues. And so we really looked at that. We have a very careful structure that's set up so that anything we do political is through a political action committee which is made up of our members acting separate from the organization. There are discussions among labor unions, women's groups, and us about third party activity building from the grass-roots locally in a third party kind of movement, and we've always been interested in discussions. We've endorsed Jesse Jackson, we worked real hard to get delegates elected to the Democratic Convention in '80 as a way to impact on what went on there trying to win more representation for low-income people within the DP [Democratic Party] to see if it was possible to turn that party around. And then recently moving in a direction in which with Jesse as kind of an interim move away from the DP as a possible third party strategy. We organized large numbers of people who feel very strongly about the way this country is going. And we see huge numbers of people everyday, every month, every year. Our point of view about America is different from the left, the people who don't ever get to experience the fact that large numbers of people want change. So we're just out there rockin' and rollin' to make a change in this country hopefully within our lifetimes. And having a wonderful time. For us the question is can we organize enough people fast enough. What we don't find is what the left has to think about or worry about all the time is whether there is anybody who feels the same way I do. We don't ever find that. It's only can we reach them all fast enough to get them organized seems to be the problem for our side. (May 1991)

Others mentioned the retrenchment and retreat into which many community organizations fell in the 1980s. This phenomenon had to do partly with the decrease in the amount of money available from the federal government (see Table 4.1) and also with the mood in the neighborhoods.

It's become, "Don't cut my program. Don't cut the police; don't cut this," as opposed to building something. Changing something. It's kind of a re-entrenchment. You can organize people around a "don't" when they're directly threatened by that "don't." For a short period of time you can move them into action around those kinds of things. But you don't build on to an extended organization that way. You mobilize people. Which is fine. I'm not saying either of those is good or bad. They're different strategies. The other pieces that are critical on that are the whole change in the federal government. The Feds with the Reagan administration have radically changed their view of the local community. You can go right to the HUD [U.S. Department of Housing and Urban Development] office and win some things.   Those have a major impact.   It has changed the ball game.   (March 1991)

In order to adjust to the changing political climate, many organizations began to push to make lending institutions accountable. In Chapter 3, a bank action in Baltimore was described; similar scenes were repeated in Detroit; Chicago; Cleveland; Washington, D.C.; Oakland, and many other cities. Three federal statutes were influenced by community organizations: the Home Mortgage Disclosure Act (HMDA) of 1975 (Public Law 94-200), the Community Reinvestment Act (CRA) (Title 8 of the Housing and Community Development Act of 1977) and the Financial Institutions Reform, Recovery and Enforcement Act (FIRREA) of 1989.   HMDA was an attempt to expose redlining practices in the lending industry. The Home Mortgage Disclosure Act enables the public to determine the geographical lending patterns of most banks and savings institutions by census tract.   This law requires banks and savings and loan institutions to submit an annual statement detailing the number, amount, and type (whether insured, conventional, or home improvement) of loans by census tract.   These reports are to be made available to the public upon request, in a regulation based on the assumption that reporting will promote more equitable lending patterns through consumer pressure.

Because of the exemptions to HMDA and, frequently, less-than-enthusiastic reporting by lending institutions, Congress continued to debate remedies for redlining.   In 1977, the Community Reinvestment Act was passed. According to the Center for Community Change, the CRA "redefines the responsibility of lending institutions to communities.   It emphasizes the continuing and affirmative obligation of lending institutions to meet credit needs and make loans as well as take deposits" (1989, 11).   According to industry commentary on the CRA, bank supervisors investigating compliance look for "a pattern of loan applications, extensions, and rejections that shows concentration in high-income areas to the general exclusion of low and moderate-income neighborhoods.   This information will be derived from records required by HMDA regulations, and when resources allow, it will be plotted on community maps to reveal the bank's lending pattern" (Healey 1979, 726).   Thus, the CRA can be used by communities as leverage for increasing lending activity in neighborhoods and to begin to ameliorate past deficiencies. However, the CRA is more than a little ambiguous.   It does not define, "meet credit needs of a community." How much is enough? Is there a ratio of deposits to loans that should be maintained? What type should the loans be? What should be the geographic parameters of a lending institution? All these questions and more are left unanswered by the law. Certainly, the onus is on local community groups to press the lending industry.

With the passage of the Financial Institutions Reform, Recovery and Enforcement Act (FIRREA) in 1989, major revisions were made in HMDA; these revisions became effective in 1990, but the new forms with the expanded data were not available until 1992. The coverage of HMDA was expanded to include other mortgage lenders besides those affiliated with depository institutions or holding companies and added mortgage companies whose assets combined with their parent company exceed $10 million; while some smaller mortgage companies will remain exempt from reporting requirements, the bulk of mortgages are made by lenders whose assets are well beyond the $10 million asset baseline. Data regarding loan applications must be reported under FIRREA, potentially providing a remedy for the problem of comparing supply and demand or request and denial. For the purpose of HMDA reporting, an application results when an institution receives an oral or written request for a mortgage or home improvement loan made in accordance with the institution's procedures. However, FIRREA requires lenders to report the race, sex, and income of mortgage applicants and borrowers; only depository institutions with assets under $30 million are exempt from this particular requirement. ("Home Mortgage Disclosure" 1989, 51357-51359).

Organizations across the country began to make CRA challenges and learned to use the new laws to pressure lending institutions to be more responsive to poor neighborhoods. An organizer observes:

Local organizations have taken advantage of national politics. For instance, there's been a lot of neighborhood activity around the Community Reinvestment Act. There are a couple of national housing institutes that were instrumental in getting a handle and a whole cross-section of local organizations have taken up CRA challenges. A variety of the organizing networks have picked up on it, most notably ACORN. There have been a number of independent efforts as well because the information is out there and the tool is there. People read about other groups making challenges. (May 1991)

Many organizations began to rethink their tactics in light of the current political milieu, and some have begun to move away from overt protests and even to talk disparagingly of those who use them.

An example, last year Levi's closed a plant in San Antonio and laid off 1,000 people. Out of that some people started organizing the Levi's workers. It was typical protest politics. We were in the beginning of developing this job training program with the same issues. Recognizing that people here are undereducated and untrained and are going to be stuck in low wage jobs in an economy where increasingly jobs, even lower level jobs, are going to require a higher level of education. That's straightforward, but for regular folks, understanding that, the implications of that—it's important. So our whole response has been to work to develop an alternative system that uses public resources directly to educate people so they can get better jobs. Levi's response, or the response of these other folks, was to protest. I went over there and talked about a job training, transition process with the Levi's people. I walk into the plant, there's 30 people there with signs, police were there, some old Socialist Worker Party guy was there yelling something. But out of that they've now built an organization where a significant number of people, very unsophisticated, mostly women have become involved in this whole organization. Their leaders are flying out to San Francisco to be in boycotts. It's just a waste of people's time and energy in my mind. Because they can't win. They cannot win. I've been to their meetings and there's really no attempt at all to help people understand what's happened, to put this in a realistic context and help them interpret what's going on. There's a lot of rhetoric about capitalism, profiteering that gets people angry and preys on the grief that they experience about unemployment. (May 1991)

Other organizers focus more on what works, that is, what is effective in bringing about concrete change:

I think it was an evaluation of what was working and what wasn't working and being able to do real strong and honest evaluation of what has worked and hasn't worked and looking at new tactics. I don't think it's progressive over time. It is your structure and what you're constituency will buy, what they'll do, what they'll become involved with. It's not only IAF. It's PICO and many other federated organizations; the number of people who are now doing organizing differently, partly because of the times. (March 1991)

Perhaps tactics have changed because the targets of more confrontational tactics are more astute in their dealings with organizations. Perhaps organizations use different actions because their targets know how to handle the old style of collective action. Most organizers reported that targets, including banks, local officials, and developers, are more subtle in their rejections of community organizations.

I don't think targets are more astute than in previous years. They are vulnerable. Everybody has some weak or vulnerable points. My experience is that for the most part targets are more subtle. They say they'll work with you. And that's more difficult to organize against. It takes some time for people to realize that sitting down at a table doesn't mean anything. It's not changing. (February 1991)

In 1974, Title 1 of the Housing and Community Development Act consolidated many programs into the Community Development Block Grants (CBDG) program. One of the latent benefits of these funds was that community groups could influence where and how the money was spent. Lobbying and writing proposals became standard fare for many groups. When the program began, there was $2.5 billion allocated for cities nationwide, and the total jumped to $3.8 billion by 1980; however, by the end of the decade, the program had been nearly decimated, and funding was far below the 1975 level (Table 4.1). The demise of the CBDG and the Urban Development Action Grants (UDAGs) is well documented. Community organizations in major cities were been affected by the change in priority during the 1980s and early 1990s. Total expenditures for the UDAGs, which were used to finance downtown development projects in Detroit, Chicago, Oakland, San Antonio, and many other cities, totaled nearly $700 million in 1980, but by 1987, the program was entirely eliminated. The block grants, which were also greatly reduced, were often used to complete downtown projects, to the detriment and exclusion of the local neighborhoods.

Many of the organizers mentioned the deleterious effect of these changes as well as of cuts in human services. "There's a big difference between organizing in 1968 and organizing in 1991. In the sixties, they physically had more money. You don't have that in the '90s. You have a great difference in activity in general" (March 1991). Others expanded on the theme of how the budget cuts have influenced the tactics in community organizing.

The resources available to community groups are almost all gone. The pie is

Table 4.1
Shrinking Aid to Cities: Budgets (in Billions) for Major Urban
Programs (Adjusted for Inflation)

Program	1981	1993	% change
Urban Development Action Grants	$0.6	$0.0	-100.0
General Revenue Sharing	8.0	0.0	-100.0
Employment and Training	14.3	4.2	-70.6
Assisted Housing	26.8	8.9	-66.8
Economic Development Administration	0.6	0.2	-66.7
Clean Water Construction	6.0	2.6	-56.7
Mass Transit	6.9	3.5	-49.3
Community Development Block Grants	6.3	4.0	-36.5

Source: U.S. Conference of Mayors Annual Report, 1994.

cut, where there is a pie. There is no more division of loose money as
there was in the '60s and '70s. The people in political power in cities
and states are cutting and not adding to. They are cutting back. The
distribution of what little resources are left is very tight. So 15 years
ago when you left for City Hall with 10 or 20 people to demonstrate to
get a program or to get something done in your neighborhood, it could
be effective because the resources were there to solve the problem.
Today, the resources aren't there. So you go in to negotiate with the
mayor and he or she says, I can't add police; I can't add firemen; I
can't fix your streets. There are no funds left. So it is much more
difficult to win those issues. (March 1991)

Some organizers mentioned the resiliency of communities of poor
people in the face of the budget crunch:

Money flowed under [President Jimmy] Carter and we enjoyed that as well as all organizations, I think. It stopped still under Reagan and we knew how to survive. It wasn't any fun, but we certainly knew how to survive. So there's no government money for organizing out there. And there certainly was under Carter. (February 1991)

Others noted that it was not just the federal government that was diminishing its support of community organizations:

Resources are an issue. It makes community organizing difficult. The delegitimizing of the approach. Big funders like the Ford Foundation don't consider community organizing a viable approach. There's less and less money. To get money for leadership training, you can't just tell people you're gonna kick a little ass and you'll get some "bennies" [benefits]. That just doesn't work anymore. (March 1991)

The budget cuts of the 1980s and 1990s have changed the face of community organizing as organizations had to scramble for funding. Not coincidentally, the shift to organizational-based community organizing started at about the same time. The strategy here is to get several organizations (often churches) to pay dues to a community organization that tackles many neighborhood issues. This method assures funding and a solid base of members but may limit the issues that the organization confronts to those issues that are deemed appropriate by the churches or other organizations.

Other organizers emphasized the international climate and its impact on community organizing in poor communities:

Frankly, I think it's more important that we think about international climate. Tip O'Neil's thing that "All politics is local," is true. That's where people's interests are, that is where they understand their world. But we're living in the middle of times of tremendous structural change and there is no way for that to be interpreted to people. The institutions, churches helped people build a framework, a context for their lives. As the world has changed and churches are struggling, unions aren't healthy—where do people go to understand their interests in the context of what's happening nationally or internationally? Unless people can understand, it's difficult for them to make sense out of what's happening. Institutions do not help people do that. The place they have is the media, but the media has no memory. By and large, events are isolated in the newspaper or on TV. The cutback in federal housing dollars affects people, and other changes in the economy have affected people drastically. Lot of changes because of the internationalization of the economy. But if they don't understand that, to make sense of it, there's no way to respond. And for those that do respond, often times their response is protest. (May 1991)

One organizer mentioned the reluctance of some organizations in connecting local issues to the larger, international political scene.

That was intentional, that wasn't an accident. There was an ideological position around localism that was in response partly to the large national programs in the sixties that failed as well as an anti-left position which was very prevalent in community organizing. People were afraid to be called communists. [The group] was red-baited not because we were nationalists, but because we were left. We took people to Nicaragua. There was not an openness in community organizing to that kind of politics. Even in more progressive places like the Midwest Academy, they weren't open for years. It wasn't until '85 or '86 when individuals went to work in the peace campaign in Washington, D.C. That opened the door for people who did citizen action to connect to international issues. There are some organizations that have always been open, but those are individual local organizations where you have a progressive staff person from Lefty politics. The organizations that have always been more open are unaffiliated, people-of-color organizations. They have a long history of politics connected with international issues. But that shit didn't come out of Jobs with Peace; that came out a local organization with a very progressive person who did that stuff on a local level. That's the politicalization of some large national organization—it came from local organizations, many of them people of color organizations. (February 1991)

CONCLUSION

In Chapter 2, I explored how the organizational construct influences the type and style of collective action employed by community organizations comprised of poor people. This chapter provides another lens through which to view collective action choices, namely, the local and national political climate. It will be remembered that in this volume, political climate includes the structure of the local governments as well as the manner in which council members or alderpersons are elected. Political climate also refers to the relationship between the community organization and the mayor, particularly including race and ethnic considerations. Finally, political climate refers to national and international policies as well as the national administration.

According to the community organizers, the structure of the

local governments does not delimit the actions of organizations comprised of poor people. While an identifiable target is still a priority for effective organizing, all organizers felt that a target could be ferreted out regardless of the local structure. However, according to most organizers, the target is still often the mayor, regardless of the structure, because he or she is generally the most visible. Using protest synonymously with riots, Eisinger (1973) did not find a relationship between the local political opportunity structure and the incidence of urban protest. In this work, collective action does not include riots but rather consists of organized and planned actions that are often tightly orchestrated. Others (e.g., Lineberry and Fowler 1967) noted that sometimes, reforms in local government (for instance nonpartisan elections, adding a city manager, and holding at-large elections) result in a lessened response to minority group demands, but they focused only on demands made in riot-like situations. This work did not find any relationship between the structure of the local political climate and the type or style of actions engaged in by poor people.

The support for partisan district elections of council members, commissioners, or alderpeople is nearly unanimous among community organizers, and many of them have spent part of their careers working for such reform. The exceptions are an organizer in Miami who preferred the non-partisan at-large elections and organizers in Detroit who are resigned to the fact that there will always be non-partisan, at-large elections for the Detroit city council.

Issues of race and ethnicity concerning the mayor and the community organizations still influence the tactics of many organizations comprised of poor people. While many organizers were quick to note that quiescence toward a perceived ally was waning, all (except one) mentioned that their constituency was less inclined toward contentious actions when there was an ally (or perceived ally) in the mayor's office.

There is no doubt that the political climate, in all the dimensions discussed here, does help to shape, and in some instances constrain, the types of collective action undertaken by poor people in the United States. However, the type of political climate determinism put forth by Piven and Cloward (1977) appears overstated as it seems to reduce participants in collective action to pawns in some meta-social chess game. "Protesters win, if they win at all, what historical circumstance has already made ready to be conceded" (1977, 36). This type of pessimism concerning movement workers is but the other side of Michels's (1949) description of protestors as incapacity of acting, incompetence of masses, incapacity for actions. There can be no doubt that the political climate may play a role in determining types of actions, but sometimes, poor people can organize to make their own history, rather than remaining passive agents.

5

Empowerment: A Third Alternative

Later, when the Tennessee National Guard wanted to take over 20,000 acres for a new base, we really got after them—demonstrations, accountability sessions, letters to the editors of papers all over the state. We beat 'em. They didn't build.   *—An Organizer*

Common American elite and intellectual understandings of the causes of poverty have typically oscillated between the poles of the individual responsibility of the poor and the adverse social circumstances that they confront (Patterson 1981). Consequently, the obvious solutions to poverty have appeared to be either efforts to improve the behavior of the poor or some form of alms. As a result, both politicians and philanthropists have continued to debate how social policies could be designed around these polar understandings to reduce poverty and mitigate its deleterious effects on individuals and communities, with the balance swinging now one way and then the other.

The poor themselves, on the other hand, have constantly—if sporadically, intermittently, and much of the time, unsuccessfully—struggled to define publicly the problem of poverty as essentially one of their own powerlessness (Piven and Cloward 1977). It has been rare that elites have done so as well, but the late 1960s and early 1970s saw politicians and philanthropists, both secular and religious, do so with great enthusiasm. Many of them vigorously pursued efforts to "empower the poor." Agents of the federal government, private foundations, and organized religious groups all developed programs to support poor groups and communities in developing strategies to help themselves.

The intent and consequences of these elite efforts have been widely debated (see Jenkins and Eckert 1986). On the one hand, many researchers have suggested that elites intervened in order to protect themselves against the consequences of a successful insurgency by the poor upon their own interests, while on the other, many have argued that the increased patronage fueled that insurgency. In addition, others have suggested that the increased patronage moderated the goals and tactics of the poor insurgents, while others have characterized the effect as one of channeling goals.

In any case, however, these elites, with the support of poor empowerment efforts, were typically short-lived. From the 1980s into the 1990s, we have witnessed an increased emphasis in the public discourse upon the individual responsibility of the poor for their own circumstances (Murray 1984; Kaus 1992). Moreover, even those who are more inclined to see poverty as the result of adversity and, therefore, to be more sympathetic with the plight of the poor have tended to argue for alms to the exclusion of renewed calls for poor empowerment (Imig 1992; Jencks 1992; Wilson 1987). By the 1980s, elite support for poor empowerment efforts had declined precipitously.

Nonetheless, local grass-roots efforts to empower the poor continue across the United States (see, for instance, Rogers 1991; Reitzes and Reitzes 1987; and Delgado, 1986). One base of consistent elite financial support for these efforts has been the Campaign for Human Development (CHD), an agency of the American Conference of Catholic Bishops. In examining the history of that support and the systematic evidence assembled about the groups that recently have received it, I provide a glimpse into the contemporary organized struggles of poor groups to change their own circumstances.

A SHORT CHRONICLE OF EFFORTS TO EMPOWER THE POOR

Poor empowerment refers to the efforts of poor people themselves, sometimes with the aid of non-poor allies, to collectively create power that can be directed toward alleviating poverty and the conditions that produce it.[1] In the twentieth century United States, these efforts have typically been based in neighborhoods, workplaces, and religious communities.

The labor movement until recently represented the most vigorous and successful of those efforts at poor empowerment (Dulles and Dubofsky 1984), with its most notable successes focused upon the workplace and coming during the late 1930s and 1940s. Moreover, the labor movement was not without its more recent successes as the emergence of a strong farmworkers movement attested (Jenkins 1985a). Neighborhood organizing efforts in the early part of the century, inspired by the Progressives, did not effectively build power or build neighborhood organizations that were either democratic or effective in combatting the causes of poverty (Fisher 1984).

The 1960s saw a burst of poor empowerment efforts, including those of the civil rights movement, based importantly in the black church (McAdam 1982; Morris 1984). It also saw some that were based in primarily in neighborhoods such as those of Saul Alinsky and the early Industrial Areas Foundation (Horwitt 1989), the Mobilization for Youth (Moynihan 1969), and those short-lived forays of the Students for a Democratic Society (Sale 1973) and the Student Nonviolent Coordinating Committee (Carson 1981). One of the most interesting poor empowerment endeavors of the 1960s, even though it was ultimately unable to survive, was the National Welfare Rights Organization (NWRO) which brought together disconnected welfare recipients in an effort to assault poverty by the collective efforts of the most deprived of the poor, welfare mothers (West 1981; Bailis 1974).

Jack Walker recently observed about poor empowerment, in concluding his study of interest group representation in Washington during the 1980s, that "Political mobilization of those at the bottom of the social order is exceedingly difficult because there are few patrons able or willing to risk the danger to their own political well-being that might arise from heavy political conflict over redistributive social programs" (1991, 196). However, for a brief period, the burst of power empowerment efforts of the 1960s and early 1970s drew the financial support of more elite patrons than usual—the early burst of what Rabinowitz (1990) has called "progressive social change philanthropy." While some researchers suggested that outside resources spurred those efforts (McCarthy and Zald 1973), most concluded that they were inspired by, and followed, the indigenous efforts of poor communities to empower themselves (Jenkins and Eckert 1986).

Jenkins (1985b), in his systematic empirical study of foundation funding of social movements, demonstrated the expanded support for progressive activities of all types by foundations during that period, including support for poor empowerment groups. Jenkins estimated that at the peak, in the early 1970s, private foundation giving to social movement organizations of all types reached $28 million; it had declined to about $12 million by 1980 (in 1967 dollars) (1985b:13). The widely noted efforts that developed out of President Lyndon Johnson's War on Poverty also led, if briefly, to support for poor empowerment efforts (Moynihan 1969). Some of the most sustained efforts came out of organized religion.

The support of NWRO by Protestant denominations, which was extensively documented by Guida West, illustrates the pattern of support:

White mainline denominations and their agencies joined [in supporting the NRWO] at all levels as early as 1966 and continued their support through the 1970s. Most were Protestant. More specifically, at the national level, the National Council of Churches, through its agency the Interreligious Foundation for Community Organization, and the United Church of Christ, though its Welfare Priority Team, became major contributors to NWRO in terms of financial, political and social resources. (West 1981, 146)

Goaded by a resuscitated social gospel that resonated with the movements of the period emphasizing the empowerment of the poor rather than alms for the poor,

IFCO was organized in the early part of 1967. The "troika" of the liberal Protestant denominations involved in urban work—the United Presbyterian church, the United Church of Christ, and the Episcopal church—conceived a plan to support community organization of the poor and set about to implement it. Later, other denominations—the Methodists and the Lutherans—joined the IFCO. (West 1981, 150)

Moreover, "the United Church of Christ [specifically the United Church Board for Homeland Ministries] provided NWRO with both material and other resources, namely money, staff, networks, media coverage, and legitimation of its cause among the liberal sector" (West 1981, 154). However, "declining support for IFCO by major denominations [forced it] to cut back on all its programs by the early 1970s" (West 1981, 154).

Lagging a bit in institutionalizing its own impulse for efforts to empower the poor in the United States, the Roman Catholic Church created the first embodiment of the Campaign for Human Development (CHD) in the early 1970s. In November 1969, the United States Catholic Bishops adopted the Resolution on the Crusade Against Poverty, which ultimately led to the creation of CHD. This resolution called for the creation of a new source of financial capital that would be allocated for specific projects aimed at eliminating the causes of poverty. These funds were to be used for organizing groups of white and minority poor people to help them develop economic strength and political power in their own communities. It was envisioned that the funds would be used to support projects such as voter registration, community organizations, nonprofit housing corporations, community-run schools, minority-owned cooperatives and credit unions, job-training programs, and rural cooperatives (National Conference of Catholic Bishops 1969).

The roots of CHD can be traced to two powerful historical events, the Second Vatican Council of the Catholic Church (Vatican II) and the social turmoil of the United States during the 1960s. The Second Vatican Council provided a theological base for the development of social justice works. Bishop Malone states that the council concluded that "the demands for justice should be given high priority, because not only the effects but also the caused of social ills must be removed. And assistance should be given in such a way that the recipients would be freed from dependence on others and would become self sufficient" (United States Catholic Conference 1986, 3).

The second major factor, the social situation in the United States during the 1960s, provided a context for applying the principles of Vatican II. By the 1960s many individuals became aware of "the other America." Despite the fact that the majority of Americans enjoyed a healthy standard of living, millions of citizens were living in poverty and millions more were surviving on the edges of poverty. The civil rights movement highlighted the extent to which systematic racism is related to poverty. As a result of the convergence of the two forces, the United States bishops determined that, in addition to the extensive traditional charitable activities of the Church, a new effort should be undertaken to address the causes of poverty, dependency and despair. Thus, in 1970, the Campaign for Human Development was established.

POOR EMPOWERMENT AND THE PROBLEM OF RESOURCES

As the discussion so far has suggested, it is assumed that relatively stable, sustained, organized efforts at poor empowerment at the grass-roots level are dependent, to some extent, upon resources drawn from outside the poor communities themselves. A recent major study of formally organized interest groups of all kinds has concluded that "a successful set of political organizations representing a constituency will not come into being, no matter how clever or energetic the leaders of the movement, unless institutions can be identified that will serve as sponsors or patrons for their efforts" (Walker 1991, 196). For non-poor communities, these patrons may be found among well-endowed constituents, but the nature of poor constituencies guarantees that patrons must come from outside the poor constituency itself. This means that groups representing the poor must seek outside resources in order to become formally organized and to survive for any period of time. Dependency upon such outside patrons is widely seen as moderating the goals and tactics of groups representing the oppressed. The consequences of this trade-off have been widely criticized (Piven and Cloward 1977), yet most poor empowerment groups come to terms with such potentially dependent ties to outside supporters (Hall 1991).

Moreover, while this chronicle of recent poor empowerment efforts suggests that the level of outside patronization has declined recently, this does not mean that its level has become insignificant. Rabinowitz, in a unique effort attempts to estimate the annual level of such outside financial support in the late 1980s, says:

About $100 million, comprising about $50 million from foundations and another $50 million from church-related activities, represents the full amount of/grants available in a typical recent year for the support of progressive social change organizations. On the average, grants from foundations and religious organizations probably amount to no more than one-third to one-half of a grantee's total annual revenue. Thus, the $100 million I have estimated as the total contribution in the form of grants leads to an estimate as the total contribution in the form of grants leads to an estimate in the order of $200-$300 million for the total revenues for the operation of progressive social change organizations at the grass-roots or community level. (Rabinowitz 1990, 31-32)

Given this dependence on patrons, the organizational requirements of those patrons that emanate from their legal tax status, it is not surprising that the majority of grass-roots poor empowerment groups are formally registered non-profits (McCarthy, Shields, and Conrad 1991).

DEMOGRAPHY OF POOR EMPOWERMENT GROUPS

The primary interest here is in describing formally organized collective action by the poor that is aimed at empowering poor communities. However, our window on this organized action results from the evidence assembled about groups supported recently by CHD. The population of groups that CHD funds is highly selected by a number of criteria beyond the potential of the specific empowerment projects they propose.

This section first describes the three data sets that were developed to characterize these groups and then provides an explanation of their structure, approach, goals, and support patterns.

DATA SETS

Three discrete data sets were used, each of which describes a different cohort of CHD-funded groups. Each annual cycle provides funds for approximately 200 local groups. Some groups are funded for more than one year, so each annual cohort includes groups that were funded in previous years as well as newly funded groups. As a result, each of these data sets includes a different, but overlapping, set of locally funded groups.

One set, the *file set*, was generated out of the CHD files and describes all the 208 groups that received funds for community organization from CHD during 1991. All the information provided to CHD by these groups in their application for funds, as well as the questionnaire they completed just prior to receiving the grants, was abstracted.

A second set, the *survey set*, was created by surveying all the groups that were funded by CHD between 1987 and 1989 (see Chapter 2). Approximately 52% of those groups responded to a questionnaire that was mailed to them soliciting information, especially concerning the tactics that they used to empower themselves.

A third set, the *assessment set*, was generated to provide information for an assessment of the activities of CHD-funded groups solicited by the United States Catholic Conference (USCC) (McCarthy, Shields and Conrad 1988; Byron 1989). In order to gather information on the experiences of those who received CHD funding, a survey questionnaire was developed and mailed to all groups that received

CHD funding for the five-year period of 1982 through 1986. A total of 426 groups were mailed questionnaires; of these, 176 questionnaires were returned, for an overall response rate of 41%. In addition to the survey, additional data on 152 of the 176 projects were systematically collected from the files of CHD.

Group Goals

Groups are selected by CHD because they profess the general goal of empowering poor communities. Their statements about how they will go about doing this (both in the file and the survey data sets) primarily stress developing indigenous leadership, organizing poor people, and building strong organizational structures. The range of specific issues that they address is rather broad (including toxic waste problems, banking services, taxation policies, transportation, environmental issues, homelessness, tenants rights, voter registration and problems of the elderly), but the majority of the groups focus their primary attention on community economic development, education, employment (jobs), affordable housing, health care issues, and minority rights. In the assessment survey, groups were asked to project the specific issues that would most occupy them in the next decade, and the issues that dominated their future vision were found to be employment, education, health, and affordable housing.

Group Age, Membership, and Staffing

Ninety-four percent of the groups funded in 1991 (file data) reported being non-profit organizations, with 86% reporting being formally incorporated. Almost identical proportions of groups responding to the assessment survey said they were non-profits and were formally incorporated (93% and 89% respectively).

It should be emphasized that these groups are of very recent vintage. For instance, 95% of the groups that Hall questioned in a survey had been founded after 1960, 90% after 1970, and 60% after 1980 (Hall 1991). The evidence from the files shows that of the groups that CHD funded in 1991, more than 50% had been founded after 1982. Moreover, the assessment data shows a similar pattern, with 61% of the groups reporting having started after 1980.

The relative youth of these organizations is illustrated when compared with a national sample of voluntary associations of all types (Knoke 1990) which reported an average age of over 30 years. The population of Washington, D.C. citizens' groups surveyed by Walker (1991) revealed, however, that half were founded after 1965, which was a period of rapid expansion of groups of that type (groups with open membership, with membership appeals unrelated to profession and focusing on broad ideals or issues). A sample of grass-roots peace movement groups (McCarthy, Britt, and Wolfson 1991) similarly shows a recent burst of group formation, with a little more than half of the groups having been founded before 1980. Apparently, the rate of formation of poor empowerment groups accelerated during the last several decades, as did the rate of formation among citizens groups of other kinds.[2]

The founding pattern that is visible here suggests that groups aimed at empowering the poor emerged, importantly, in response to the opportunities that were created by the expansion of "outside support" for poor empowerment during the 1960s and early 1970s. And, while this period saw the rapid expansion of non-profit as well as profit groups (Walker 1991; Coleman 1982), this population of poor empowerment groups is strikingly young.

Describing the membership size and composition of these groups is not as straightforward as it might seem to the casual observer. About one-third of the poor empowerment groups are organizations of organizations, in that they do not enroll members directly but rather affiliate constituent organizations and groups, a strategy of organization building called *bloc recruiting* (Oberschall 1973). This is a common, if not widely recognized, organizational form among citizens groups (Walker 1991). The median number of organizational members for the poor empowerment groups with such members was 17 (mean = 71) in the assessment data. Typically, these organizations of organizations report the total membership of their constituent groups when asked for membership figures. Groups that enroll the members of pre-existing groups, such as neighborhood groups, congregations, and tenants groups, can more easily build large memberships than those that recruit members individually.

All the groups have at least one paid staff member. The file data set shows a range of 1 to 37 paid staff, with a mean number of staff of 6.25. The groups reported 26% of the staff to be African-American and 34%, Hispanic. The assessment evidence, representing an earlier cohort of funded groups, shows a range of 1 to 9 paid staff, with a median of 3. The survey data also reveal that all organizations have at least 1 paid staff member. Nearly 40% of the organizations reported that the annual salary of the director or, in some cases, the lead organizer is less than $15,000. Less than 10% of the directors are paid in excess of $35,000.

Given the typically very small number of paid staff in these groups, they depend heavily on volunteer leadership and efforts to carry out organizational tasks and the work of trying to bring about change on issues. This contrasts sharply with the trend in national-level citizens groups,where professional paid staff are increasingly responsible for these tasks.

Group Governance and Decision-Making

Almost all the groups have a board of directors of some form, but this is not surprising given the importance of responsible boards within the non-profit community (McCarthy, Britt, and Wolfson 1991). Over 60% of the boards are elected by the membership of the group, with the bulk of the rest reporting self-perpetuating boards where members are appointed by the board itself (survey data set). Most of the groups have formally designated officers, somewhat more than half have officers elected by the membership, and the bulk of the rest have officers appointed by the board of directors (survey data set).

Most of the groups have task committees that are responsible for one or another of the chores of maintaining a struggling community organization. The most prevalent is a fundraising committee (63% of the groups report having one), but 45% of the groups have a membership committee, 38% have a program committee, 31% have a committee that helps in setting organizational goals and 22% have a publicity committee (survey data set). There is considerable difference in organizational differentiation as measured by the number of committees. Nearly 13% of the 187 organizations that responded to Hall's questionnaire reported that their organization has no committees, while 11.8% noted that they had five or more committees as part of the organizational structure.

Organizational Capacity

An important issue facing all community organizations is organizational capacity, the degree to which organizations are able to develop and integrate within their structures elements that will enhance their ability to be effective in attaining specific goals and objectives. Organizational capacity focuses, not on specific outcomes such as the number of affordable housing units developed in a neighborhood or the number of jobs created because of the efforts of a community organization, but rather on elements of organizational development.

Using data from the assessment file, seven different dimensions of capacity for organizational development were identified: (1) indigenous leadership, (2) fundraising capabilities, (3) group empowerment strategies, (4) leadership support, (5) coalitions, (6) community support, and (7) organizational structure.

These seven dimensions were arrived at empirically by factor-analyzing a bank of questions that focused on self-evaluations of organizational capacity (Shields 1991). Table 5.1 contains descriptive statistics on these measures.

The findings of this analysis show that the community organizations rate themselves as being most effective at developing group empowerment strategies and indigenous leadership and least effective at developing fundraising capabilities and leadership financial responsibility. These findings further indicate how vulnerable these organizations are with regard to financial issues.

Group Finances

The major sources for the revenue that these groups raise to carry out their efforts to empower the poor reveal both the focus of their own fundraising efforts as well as what we might call the "financial opportunity structure" that they face in seeking patronage. Moreover, while financial resources are crucial to the survival of many of these groups, 96% of them reported that "people" were one of their two most important resources, while only 33% of the groups reported that money was one of their two most important resources (survey data set). I can paraphrase Bell (1976) by proposing that the budget of a poor empowerment group is the skeleton of the organization stripped of all misleading ideologies.

Table 5.1
Measures of Organizational Capacity

Capacity Type	Mean*
Development of group empowerment	5.99
Development of indigenous leadership	5.96
Development of coalitions	5.90
Development of community support	5.80
Development of organizational structure	5.40
Development of fundraising capabilities	5.07
Development of leadership financial responsibility	4.62

*Capacity type sub-scales vary in number and items. This score represents the mean score of all items on a 1 to 7 scale, with 7 being the highest self-rating.

Table 5.2 displays the major sources of revenue reported for the year 1990 for CHD groups funded in 1991. The average budget reported by these groups in 1990 was $211,382. In the survey of organizations that received funds from CHD from 1987 through 1989, the average budget was $173,000. The grants and donations category and the government grant category accounted for the largest amounts of revenue across all groups, but it may be observed that a minority of groups actually received government grants. Those that did received relatively large amounts, however. More than 90% of the groups reported revenue from grants and grass-roots fundraising, which was the most common source of revenue for these groups. This evidence makes clear the dependence of grass-roots poor empowerment groups on outside patrons. Extensive efforts at grass-roots fundraising produce only a little more than 10% of the total revenue for these groups in the past fiscal year. However, recall that these figures are based upon each groups' report for the fiscal year prior to their receipt of a 1991 grant. A substantial number of them received their first CHD grant in 1991. Based on the survey responses, the percentage of the groups's funding that comes from external sources is quite a bit lower than the figures shown in Table 5.2.[3]

Table 5.2
Organizational Revenue Sources for Poor Empowerment CHD Groups (1990) by Major Category

Revenue Category	Percentage of a Group's Total Budget	Percentage of Groups Reporting Any Revenue from Source
Grants and donations	33.8	94.0
Government grants	29.7	39.0
Grassroots fundraising	11.8	93.0
CHD	73.0	100.0
In-kind donations	7.4	67.0
Other	7.0	62.0
TOTAL	101.1*	

Note: Total mean organizational Budget = \$211,382; $N = 198$.
*Percentages do not sum to 100% due to rounding.

The reason for this contrast is straightforward and speaks to CHD's success in encouraging the groups it funds to become more reliant upon grass-roots funding. In order to supplement the estimates generated from those reports, the budgets that each group submitted to CHD for the period they received CHD funds were reviewed. The resulting estimates suggest that for groups funded from 1987 through 1989, 61% (the mean) of their budget came from external sources, and the mean percentage of the external funding that came from the CHD grant was 31%. This is indirect evidence that the CHD-funded groups actually decreased their dependence on external sources of funds subsequent to receiving CHD funds.

Table 5.3 disaggregates the reported revenue from all non-

Table 5.3
Major Grant Sources and Percentage of Total Grant Dollars from Each Source for Poor Empowerment Groups (1990)

Grant Source	Percentage of Total	Percentage of non-CHD
Campaign for Human Development	19	---
Religious-Catholic	4	5
Religious-Protestant[a]	17	21
Foundation	29	36
Business	2	3
Non-profit organization	4	5
Community funds	2	3
Local, state, national government[b]	13	16
Other[c]	9	11
Total (%)	99*	100
Total ($)	$13,237,000	$10,708,000

[a] Protestant except for several small Jewish grants.

[b] Some government grants are reported under the grant and donation category in Table 5.2. Consequently, the estimate of governmental grants in Table 5.2 is something of an underestimate.

[c] Includes unspecified and unidentifiable donors.

*Percentages do not sum to 100 due to rounding.

governmental grant sources, as reported in Table 5.2. Each grant was coded by the nature of its source. Grants from religious sources make up the largest proportion.   Including the Campaign for Human Development grants, 40% of the grant revenue reported by these groups in 1990 came from religious sources.   Catholic and Protestant giving appears to be about even, assuming that using CHD-funded groups as our window on funding somewhat over-estimates the level of Catholic giving. Foundation revenue makes up the largest single source for these groups.

Table 5.4 disaggregates the grass-roots fundraising revenue reported by the CHD groups in 1990.   Groups listed additional donation sources as the result of grass-roots fundraising, which make up the largest category for this source (34%). Membership dues made up 30% of the grass-roots revenue that the groups raised. Recalling that grass-roots sources are reported to account for about 12% of these groups' total revenues, we can conclude that membership dues accounted for less than 5% of the revenue raised by these poor empowerment groups.

Table 5.4
Major Grass-roots Fundraising Sources and
Percentage of Total Dollars from Each Source (1990)

Grass-roots Fundraising Source	Percentage of Total Dollars
Activities (dinners, parties, raffles)	15
Membership dues	30
Local donations	34
Direct mail and canvassing	7
Telemarketing	5
Advertising books	6
Product sales	2
Other	1
TOTAL	100

Group fundraising activities, such as dances, banquets, raffles, picnics, special days, runs, variety shows, New Years celebrations, and the like accounted for 15% of the grass-roots funds raised. However, despite the rapid growth of the use of direct mail, canvassing and telemarketing by citizens groups (Oliver and Marwell 1992; Everett 1992), these groups do not raise as much from all these sources combined (12%) as they do from membership dues. The use of advertizing books—whereby local businesses, individuals and organizations are solicited to buy an advertizement in a booklet that is produced by the group to publicize its own efforts—is not uncommon among the groups (about 10% use them), but they raise rather small amounts. Product sales are not very common; they usually consist of T-shirt and button sales and do not raise much in the way of revenue. Organizations do differ in the method of collecting membership dues. Some do direct mailings to members, while others collect membership dues at meetings. Still other organizations, including ACORN, undertake their dues collecting via door-to-door canvassing. The style of collecting dues may influence the intensity of participation in the organization.[4]

Comparing the pattern of sources of revenues described here with the pattern reported by Walker (1991, 82) for a sample of Washington, D.C.-based national citizens groups is instructive. Close to half the revenues of those groups come from member contributions, in stark contrast to the small proportion of funds stemming from members of the poor empowerment groups. Most of those citizens groups, however, are made up of non-poor citizens who are able to provide financial support to maintain groups that represent their preferences for change. In contrast, the poor empowerment groups are far more dependent on patrons for financial support.

Group Tactics

Organizing the poor is not an end in itself but rather the means toward developing influence for poor groups so that their needs can be given more weight in public decision making. There are many ways in which such groups may try to influence the decision making process. Critics have suggested that heavy dependence on outside patrons will tend to moderate the tactics of groups such as these.

"Insider tactics" of legislative and administrative lobbying tend to require high levels of skilled labor which are likely to be scarce among these groups, but as Table 5.5 shows, the groups reported (survey data set) high levels of local "grass-roots lobbying" (for example, letter writing) as well as conventional lobbying of local officials and local legislative activity. Nevertheless, the groups also reported relatively high levels of "outsider tactics" such as demonstrating and picketing. These tactics have the advantage of being

Table 5.5
Tactics Reported by Poor Empowerment Groups as Having Been Used to Achieve Goals (1990)

Tactic	Percent reporting use of tactic	
	Last year	Ever
Letter writing	72	
Lobbying local funding/ government agencies	71	73
Public demonstrations	55	64
Sit-ins	9	
Civil disobedience	8	17
Building coalitions	82	
Changing local ordinances	51	
Street theater		15
Picketing		45
Boycotting		18
N	185	145

volunteer labor-intensive and relatively inexpensive—an ideal combination for these groups. This evidence suggests that these groups make rather heavy use of what have been called "unruly" tactics. A study of national-level citizens groups reported a far rarer use of demonstrations than the level reported here (Schlozman and Tierney 1986).

Finally, these groups were asked if they had ever been denied funds on account of their use of "public actions," and only 19% of the groups reported that they had. We can interpret this figure as remarkably low given the high rate of use of unruly tactics employed by these groups and their heavy dependence on outside patronage. Moreover, we can also interpret the figure as indicating the potential costs of pursuing change with public action tactics, demonstrating the vulnerability of poor people's groups.

Most studies on poor people's organizations (Valocchi 1990; Barnes 1987; Delgado 1986; Piven and Cloward 1977; Helfgot 1974; Donovan 1973) have focused, justifiably, on the deleterious effects of public policy on the poor and their organizations. The budget cuts of the 1980s and the decrease in Community Development Block Grant funding for cities is well known. The contention here is that occasionally, the causal direction is reversed, meaning that sometimes, poor people's SMOs have a strong influence on public policy.

CONCLUSION

The description of poor empowerment groups has emphasized their common features, but they are actually incredibly diverse in the goals they pursue and the ways in which they organize themselves and act collectively. Nevertheless, they share several important features. They are based in poor communities so that they advocate their own interests. As a result, they are somewhat dependent on outside patrons for the financial resources that are necessary to supplement the human resources on which they draw to bring about change. This dependence does not seem to severely curtail their use of disruptive and unruly tactics in their pursuit of empowerment. Against great odds, many of these groups have been successful in producing structural change that has positive effects on the circumstances of their own constituents.

The American Catholic Bishops have remained firm during the last two decades in the financial support of poor empowerment through the Campaign for Human Development. When CHD was launched in 1970, Bishop Dempsey said, "We have done a dangerous thing: we've created in the hearts of the poor a hope in the Catholic Church" (United

States Catholic Conference 1988). Almost 20 years later Bishop Mugavero said, "We have committed ourselves to continue to wage war against poverty using the campaign as our vehicle. We think it provides a model that sets high standards for similar efforts" (Byron 1989).

NOTES

1. Poor empowerment groups are defined, operationally, by their goals (creating power for the poor) as well as their social composition (being composed primarily of poor people themselves). As a result, what are commonly called *advocacy groups*--those that seek to help or empower the poor but are staffed or membered by the non-poor--fall outside our view. So, too, do community self-help groups (Milofsky 1988), unless they are composed primarily of poor people, as well as neighborhood organizations not made up of poor people, for example, those described by Fisher (1984) as having surged during the 1950s.

2. Community-based organizations (CBOs) have recently become one of the fastest growing types of non-profit organizations. While there is some overlap between CBOs and what are here called poor empowerment groups, probably only a small minority of CBOs are also poor empowerment groups.

3. The 1990 file data is likely the most accurate report of the annual budgets since it consists of a detailed accounting of the just-completed fiscal year. The survey is based on general estimates.

4. Everett (1992), in a detailed analysis of door-to-door canvassing as an organizational approach, suggests that the consequences of solicitation on the solicitors' organizational commitment is ambiguous, but that the level of member donor commitment is typically quite modest.

6

Conclusion

The organizational empowerment model of collective action shows that several organizational features influence the choice of tactics made by SMOs. Size has a small but significant influence, most likely because larger groups have a greater number of potential participants for any action. If members choose the tactics the SMO tends to be more contentious, at least in poor people's SMOs. Moreover, organizations that ask members to demonstrate commitment by paying dues are more likely to engage in contentious actions. In addition, groups that are either formally or informally related to other SMOs are much more likely to be contentious. The various ways in which these frequently contentious groups compete were explored. Organizational empowerment was coupled with political climate to illumine the influence of climate on tactical decisions made by SMOs.

In spite of these conclusions, one might respond, Has anything new been learned about collective action? Does this research have any real relevance for the social movement-collective behavior field? Is there any benefit for the diaspora of small, struggling social movement organizations? Are the findings here transferable to other social movements besides the poor people's movement? Where do we go from here?

Research on collective action is enhanced by the analysis of the types of tactics used. The Midwest organization that went to the hometown of the owner of the professional football team was not doing a symbolic action; rather, the intent was to procure a political advantage. Likewise, the bank action in Baltimore was not undertaken to get attention or increase membership but rather to win concessions from the lending industry. By emphasizing that many poor people's groups both form organizations and use disruptive tactics, the pernicious proposition of Piven and Cloward (1977) that groups of poor people cannot effectively organize and use oppositional tactics is called into question. Piven and Cloward assert that permanent membership organizations are counterproductive because poor people lack the expertise necessary to construct permanent organizations and time spent building organizations detracts from time that could be spent mobilizing and disrupting. Certainly, formalized organization is not a prerequisite for mass defiance, and there were some short-term concessions to the Welfare Rights Organization that resulted in quiescence.

However, the major flaw is the assertion that formalized organization is inherently incompatible with defiance. Gamson's (1990a) data showed that there is a positive relation between the degree of organization and unruliness. Similarly, Jenkins and Perrow (1977) notes that the United Farm Workers' Union has made effective use of a formalized organization and led numerous successful mass strikes. This work also reports clearly that formal organization is not necessarily an impediment to contentious action. For many of the groups in this sample of social movement organizations, the facts are that they organize, disrupt, and endure. No doubt, the funding source is crucial, but once that variable has been controlled, organization does not necessarily foster quiescence.

FUTURE RESEARCH

Interest in social movements and collective behavior has skyrocketed in the past 15 years. The social movement-collective behavior section of the American Sociological Association now boasts well over 400 members. Based on this study, what are some of the areas that should be explored?

One area for future research is the role of social movements in general, and poor people's organizations in particular, in shaping public policy. Can these organizations, or the movement, generate enough clout to change policy? Many recent writings about the poor have presented sobering accounts of how the policies of the past few years have affected them. What may be revealing is how much policy the poor have been able to change, how many homes have been built, how many jobs have been created, and how many apartments have been renovated on a minuscule amount of money. The influence in recent years of poor people on public policy, when acting through social movement organizations, is largely unchartered water.

Second, a comparative analysis of poor people's movements in this country and similar groups in other countries would be edifying. Structural and state differences could be noted, as well as similarities in local-level political structures. Similar organizational variables could be related to tactical decisions.

A third consideration is the role of gender in the leadership and constituency of SMOs. The gender influence would be interesting to examine in relation to organizational structure. It would also be interesting to discover if gender influences the type and style of collective action independent of organizational variables and the political climate of the SMO.

Finally, greater interest should be shown to the differences between organizations that persist and those that go out of business. A longitudinal study that traces the cycle of initiation, growth, decline, and decay is needed. Differences in organizational construct, local political climate, and collective action tactics might enable organizations to prolong their lives and facilitate more astute grant giving on the part of organizations like the Campaign for Human Development.

POINTS TO CONSIDER

There are several, rather operational conclusions that may be drawn from this study that are of use to community organizers as well as researchers wanting to advance this work. They are offered as parting comments.

1. The trend in social movement organizations is away from single issue organizing and toward confronting a whole spectrum of issues. It is not clear at this point whether this trend holds for all social movements or only the particular social movement—empowerment of the poor—under consideration here. Both the survey data and the personal interviews reveal this proclivity toward large, multi-purpose, umbrella organizations. For many of the organizations, the specific issues and goals come from countless hours of one-to-one or one-to-two conversations in people's living rooms, on front stoops,

and in the parks. The issues are not articulated by a single charismatic leader but rather resonate within the neighborhood.

2. As organizations increase in size, as measured by membership, the likelihood of engaging in contentious actions increases. For poor people's organizations, the primary source of power is people, and apparently, this power translates into a propensity to use confrontive tactics.

3. This work also found that the more control the rank and file have over the organizations, as measured by who selects officers, board members, and actions, the more likely the organization is to use contentious actions. It is not clear if this finding would hold for all types of social movement organizations or whether it is peculiar to poor people's movements. Most poor people have been to countless nonproductive meetings, experienced numerous broken promises, and danced the "bureaucratic shuffle." When they control their organization, they are prone to act.

4. As an organization increases its relations with other, similar social movement organizations, the tendency to use tactics that are contentious increases. The shared identity and, perhaps, shared resources are forms of empowerment which may embolden the organizations. Confrontive tactics that work (specifically those that result in a political advantage to the dissenting group) may be shared between groups or, perhaps, originate in joint strategy sessions. To organizers, this suggests strong support for consciously fostering networks between SMOs. Local social movement organizations may not be aware of the vast network of SMOs scattered throughout the country. Works like this may expand the network and help a broader-based coalition to coalesce. The role of networks among various community organizations may thus be enhanced, with more direct and confrontive actions being the result.

5. The amount of external funding that a movement organization receives does not influence the tactical choices of the group. Any analysis of the effect of external resources must include a description of the goals of the funding source and the history of the groups that the sponsoring organization funds. Thus, the acceptance of external funding is not a crossing of the Rubicon toward quiescent action. The goals and history of the funding agency are crucial to understanding the relationship between external funding and tactical considerations. Other religious and benevolent funding sources may want to consider poor people's community organizations. With the

continual wave of "self-help" ideology washing up on the shores of the country, certainly, community organizing is an acceptable craft for institutional change.

Appendices

APPENDIX A: SURVEY OF LOCAL COMMUNITY ORGANIZATIONS

Except for questions requiring a written response, please answer by drawing a circle around the numeral by your choice.

1. What is the name of your organization? _____
2. What year was the organization formed? _____
3. Does the group keep a formal membership list?
   - 1 YES
   - 2 NO
4. Does the group have a charter, constitution, or by-laws?
   - 1 YES
   - 2 NO
5. Which of the following does your organization have? (May circle more than one.)
   - 1 Paid staff
   - 2 Volunteer staff
   - 3 Officers
   - 4 Members
6. Number of members? _____
7. Does your organization have regularly scheduled meetings?
   - 1 YES
   - 2 NO

8. If yes, how often do you meet?

    1 Monthly

    2 Bimonthly

    3 Quarterly

    4 Other _____

9. On average, how many members attend? _____

10. Does your organization have a Board of Directors?

    1 YES

    2 NO (Go to Question #16)

11. If yes, how are they chosen?

    1 Elected by membership

    2 Appointed by the organization's board

    3 Appointed by local government agency

    4 Appointed by some group outside the organization (other than local government)

    5 Self-appointed

    6 Other (please specify)

_____

12. How many Board members are there?

    1 5 or fewer

    2 6-10

    3 11-15

    4 16 or more

13. What is the race/ethnic status of the Board: number in each category.

    _____   White

    _____   Afro-American

    _____   Hispanic

    _____   Native American

    _____   Other_____

14. What is the gender of Board members: number in each category.

    _____   Female

    _____   Male

15. What is the age of the Board members: number in each category.

    _____   20-30

    _____   31-40

    _____   41-50

    _____   51-60

    _____   61-70

16. Does your organization have officers?

    1 YES

    2 NO (Go to Question #22)

17. If yes, which of the following do you have?

YES	NO	
1	2	President
1	2	Vice-President
1	2	Secretary
1	2	Treasurer
1	2	Other_____

18. If yes, how are they chosen?

    1 Elected by membership

    2 Appointed by the organization's board

    3 Appointed by local government agency

    4 Appointed by some group outside the organization (other than local government)

    5 Self-appointed

19. What is the race/ethnic status of the officers: number in each category.

    _____ White

    _____ Afro-American

    _____ Hispanic

    _____ Native American

    _____ Other _____

20. What is the gender of the officers: number in each category.

    _____ Female

    _____ Male

21. What is the age of the officers: number in each category.

    _____ 20-30

    _____ 31-40

    _____ 41-50

    _____ 51-60

    _____ 61-70

22. Which of the following committees does your organization have? (May circle more than one.)

YES	NO	
1	2	Membership
1	2	Program
1	2	Fund-raising
1	2	Publicity
1	2	Goal setting
1	2	Other_____

Now I want to ask some questions about the goals and strategies of the
organization.

23. What is the primary purpose of the organization?
24. In this last year, how has your organization tried to achieve its goals?

YES	NO	
1	2	Letter writing
1	2	Lobbying local funding/govt agencies
1	2	Public demonstrations
1	2	Sit-ins
1	2	Civil disobedience
1	2	Build coalitions
1	2	Changing local ordinances
1	2	Other _____

25. Does your group ever do a public action?

    1 YES

    2 NO (Go to Question #36)

26. If yes, what public actions does your group do?

YES	NO	
1	2	Civil disobedience
1	2	Demonstrations
1	2	Street theater
1	2	Mass lobbying at local or state government offices
1	2	Picketing
1	2	Boycott
1	2	Threaten boycott
1	2	Other_____

27. How do you decide to do a public action?

YES	NO	
1	2	Vote of membership
1	2	Vote of officers
1	2	Director decides
1	2	Other _____

28. How does your group prepare for a public action?

YES	NO	
1	2	Contact other groups for support
1	2	Meetings to prepare participants
1	2	Send press releases
1	2	Other _____

29. Have funds to your organization ever been denied because the
group or a member of the group engaged in a collective action?

    1 YES

    2 NO

Who withdrew the funds? _____

How much was withdrawn? _____

30. Has anyone in your group ever been arrested for civil disobedience in connection with the group's goals?

    1 YES
    2 NO

If yes, how many times? _____
How many were arrested? _____
When was the issue? _____
What was the issue? _____
What was the action? _____
What was the media coverage?

YES	NO	
1	2	Television
1	2	Newspaper
1	2	Radio
1	2	All of the above
1	2	No media coverage
1	2	Other_____

31. Has your group ever invited media to cover your actions?

    1 YES
    2 NO

32. Do you get media coverage?

    1 YES
    2 NO

33. If yes, how often?

    1 Weekly
    2 Monthly
    3 Less than six (6) times per year
    4 More than six (6) times per year

34. Which media cover your group? (May circle more than one.)

YES	NO	
1	2	Television
1	2	Newspaper
1	2	Radio
1	2	Other_____

35. How many press releases has your group issued in the last 12 months?

    1 More than 6
    2 3-5
    3 2 or less
    4 None
    5 None in last 12 months, but did before
    6 Never issued press releases

36. If your groups does not do public actions, why not?

    1 Not effective
    2 Membership not comfortable with public actions
    3 Get what we want without public actions
    4 Other _____

1 Not effective
2 Membership not comfortable with public
   actions
3 Get what we want without public actions
4 Other

---

37. What do you view as your most important resource? Order by degree of importance with 1 = most important, 2 = second most important, etc.

_____ Money
_____ Political connections
_____ People
_____ History of success
_____ Media connections

38. What economic benefits have resulted from your organization? Please include number in each category where you circle YES.

YES	NO	
1	2	Houses renovated _____
1	2	Jobs created _____
1	2	Rent control _____
1	2	Businesses started _____
1	2	Other _____

39. Have these economic benefits occurred with the help of other organizations?

1 YES
2 NO

If yes, please describe this cooperation.

40. What non-economic benefits have resulted from your organization?

YES	NO	
1	2	Reduced crime
1	2	Better neighborhood services (please specify)_____
1	2	Stopped redevelopment projects
1	2	Increased access to health care

41. Have these non-economic benefits occurred with the help of other organizations?

1 YES
2 NO

If yes, please describe this cooperation.

42. In what ways does your group relate to similar community organizations in your area? (May circle more than one.)

YES	NO	
1	2	Attend each other's meetings
1	2	Have joint meeting(s)

1	2	Attend area-wide rallies
1	2	Support other organization's public demonstrations
1	2	Attend other organizations's public demonstrations
1	2	Lobby jointly
1	2	Write joint letters
1	2	Plan strategy together
1	2	Other _____

43. Do you publish a newsletter?
   1 YES
   2 NO

44. If yes, how often?
   1 Monthly
   2 Bimonthly
   3 Quarterly
   4 Yearly
   5 Other _____

45. To whom do you send your newsletter? (May circle more than one).

YES	NO	
1	2	Members
1	2	Other community groups
1	2	Local/state politicians

Now I want to ask about financial aspects of your organization.

46. What is the total annual budget for your organization?

47. What are the organization's sources of funding?

YES	NO	
1	2	Dues from members
1	2	Community collection
1	2	Grants
1	2	Private donor(s)
1	2	Other _____

48. How much are yearly dues for
   _____ Individuals
   _____ Groups
   _____ Corporations
   _____ Do not have dues

49. Is the position of president (director) a paid position?
   1 YES
   2 NO

50. If yes, what is the annual salary?
   1   Less than $15,000
   2    $15-19,999

5 $30-34,999
6 Over $35,000

Now a few questions about when the organization began.

53. How many members were in the organization when it was formed?_____
54. Did the organization have officers when it first began?

    1 YES
    2 NO (Go to Question #57)

55. If yes, which of the following did you have?

YES	NO	
1	2	President
1	2	Vice-President
1	2	Secretary
1	2	Treasurer
1	2	Other _____

56. If yes, how were they chosen?

    1 Elected by membership
    2 Appointed by the organization's board
    3 Appointed by local government agency
    4 Appointed by some group outside the organization (other than local government)
    5 Self-appointed

57. Did the organization have a Board?

    1 YES
    2 NO (Go to Question #60)

58. If yes, how were they selected?

    1 Elected by membership
    2 Appointed by the organization's board
    3 Appointed by local government agency
    4 Appointed by some group outside the organization (other than local government)
    5 Self-appointed
    6 Other _____

59. How many board members were there?

    1 5 or fewer
    2 6-10
    3 11-15
    4 16 or more

60. What was the goal of the organization when it was founded?
61. At that time, how did the organization try to achieve its goals?

YES	NO	
1	2	Letter writing
1	2	Lobbying local funding/govt agencies
1	2	Public demonstrations
1	2	Sit-ins

1	2	Civil disobedience
1	2	Other _____

62. When the organization began, what were the sources of funding?

YES	NO	
1	2	Dues from members
1	2	Community collection
1	2	Grants
1	2	Private donor(s)
1	2	Other_____

63. If your organization had dues, how much were yearly or initial dues for

_____ individuals

_____ groups

_____ corporations

64. When the organization began, which committees did you have?

1	Membership
2	Program
3	Fund-raising
4	Publicity
5	Goal setting
6	Other _____

Now a few questions on power.

65. How does your group define power?

1	Able to raise funds
2	Achieve our goals
3	Other groups join us in actions
4	Get a lot of press
5	Can influence local politics (please specify) _____

66. If your group currently does not have the power you want, how can it be achieved?

67. Over whom or what would your group like to have power? (May circle more than one.)

YES	NO	
1	2	Local politicians
1	2	Housing authority
1	2	Landlords
1	2	Business owners
1	2	Other _____

68. How will you know you have power?

69. Finally, how does your group measure its success?

70. What position in the organization did your current president (director) have in the organization two (2) years ago?

1	Officer
2	Committee member
3	Member at large
4	Not in organization
5	Other _____

71. What position in the organization did your current vice-president have in the organization two (2) years ago?

        1 Officer
        2 Committee member
        3 Member at large
        4 Not in organization
        5 Other _____

72. Is training given to newly elected officers?

        1 YES
        2 NO

73. If yes, who trains the newly elected officers/director?

        1   Outgoing officers
        2   A local consultant
        3   Leaders from other local community organizations
        4   Other _____

74. What are the past leaders/presidents/board members of your organization doing now? (May circle more than one.)

YES	NO	
1	2	Still in organization
1	2	Involved with other groups (please specify) _____
1	2	Have positions in local government
1	2	Other _____

How would you rank each of the following on a scale of 1 to 5?
1 = not important
5 = very important

	Rank
1. Building coalitions with other groups	
2. Getting media coverage for your organization's events	
3. Having economic goals (jobs created, rents reduced, houses rehabilitated)	
4. Having non-economic goals (better community services, reduce crime, stop city development)	
5. Attending local government meetings (city council, planning board, zoning hearings)	
6. Having a 3 year plan for the organization	
7. Training new officers	
8. Having attainable goals	
9. Having well-defined goals	
10. Doing public action (civil disobedience, demonstrations, sit-ins)	

APPENDIX B: STRUCTURED INTERVIEW QUESTIONS

I. Origin of the Organization
    Reasons
    Precipitating event
    Original goals

II. How long been director/organizer? What did you do before?

III. How long was the tenure of the previous organizer?

IV. What did you do before working here? Why organizing?

V. In the survey you mentioned that your goals are
    _____? What does this mean? Flesh it out a bit.

VI. In the survey you mentioned you do the following
     actions_____? Why these? Why not others?

VII. What is the purpose of your actions?

VIII. How does the political climate in your city or county shape what
       kind of actions you do or do not do? Any change in
       relationship with mayor and or city council in the past
       few years?

IX. Do you feel that the types of actions that groups like yours do
     have changed over the years? (more/less strident more/less
     effective) If so how and why.

X. How about the change in national politics, what has been its
    impact on community organizing? How? What about its impact
    on types of actions?

XI. What is the current state of community organizing?

XII. Is it easier/more difficult to organize now? Why?

XIII. How long would you imagine being in community organizing? Is
       this your career? What is next for you?

XIV. Is this an umbrella organization? What if any relations to a
      national or regional group or organization?

APPENDIX C: PERSONS INTERVIEWED AND THEIR AFFILIATION

Walter Davis — Southern Empowerment Project, Maryville, Tennessee

Gary Delgado — Center for Third World Organizing (CTWO), former Welfare Rights and ACORN Organizer, Oakland and Berkeley, California

Maggie DeSantis — Warren-Conner Development Coalition, Detroit, Michigan

Carol Ford — Save Our Cumberland Mountains (SOCUM), Jacksboro, Tennessee

Tom Gaudette — Midamerica Institute for Development and former co-worker with Saul Alinsky, Chicago, Illinois

John Gaventa — Highlander School, New Market, Tennessee

Holly Holcombe — People Acting in Community Together (PACT), Miami, Florida

Tom Holler — Communities Organized for Public Service (COPS), San Antonio, Texas

Keith Kelleher — Chicago Homecare Organizing Project, Chicago, Illinois

Spence Limbocker — Associate Director, Campaign for Human Development (CHD), Washington, D.C. and former organizer with Mission Coalition Organization, San Francisco, California

Myrna Melgar — St. Peter's Housing Center, San Francisco, California

Bob Meridith — Save Our Cumberland Mountains (SOCUM), Jacksboro, Tennessee

Art Potter — Michigan Avenue Community Organization (MACO), Detroit, Michigan

Rinku Sen — Center for Third World Organizing (CTWO), Oakland, California

Ed Shurna	Interfaith Organizing Project, Chicago, Illinois
Ron Snyder	Oakland Community Organization, Oakland, California
Madeline Talbot	Association for Community Reform Now (ACORN), Chicago, Illinois
Glen Warn	Messiah Housing Corporation, Detroit, Michigan
Ronald White	CHD, Washington, D.C.

References

Agnew, John. 1978. "Market Relations and Locational Conflict in Cross-National Perspective." In *Urbanization and Conflict in Market Societies*, edited by K. Cox. Chicago: Maaroufa Press.

Alinsky, Saul D. 1965. *Reveille for Radicals*. New York: Vintage.

Bailis, Lawrence Neil. 1974. *Bread or Justice: Grassroots Organizing in the Welfare Rights Movement*. Lexington, MA: D.C. Heath.

Barnes, Donna. 1987. "Organization and Radical Protest: An Antithesis?" *The Sociological Quarterly* 28:575-594.

Barnett, William P. 1990. "The Organizational Ecology of a Technological System." *Administrative Science Quarterly* 35:31-60.

Barnett, William P., and Terry L. Amburgey. 1990. "Do Larger Organizations Generate Stronger Competition?" In *Organizational Evolution—New Directions*, edited by Jitendra V. Singh. Newbury Park, CA: Sage Publications.

Baum, Joel A. C., and Christine Oliver. 1991. "Institutional Linkages and Organizational Mortality." *Administrative Science Quarterly* 36:187-218.

Bell, Daniel. 1976. *The Cultural Contradictions of Capitalism*. New York: Basic Books.

Benford, Robert, and Scott Hunt. 1992. "Dramaturgy in Social Movements: The Social Construction and Communication of Power." *Sociological Inquiry* 62:36-55.

Birnbaum, Pierre. 1988. *States and Collective Action: The European Experience*. Cambridge: Cambridge University Press.

Boyte, Harry. 1980. *The Backyard Revolution*. Philadelphia: Temple

University Press.

___. 1989. *Commonwealth*. New York: Free Press.

Brand, Karl. 1985. *Neue Soziale Bewegungen in West Europa und den USA*. Frankfurt, Germany: Campus.

Brischetto, Robert, and Rodolfo de la Garza. 1985. *The Mexican American Electorate: Public Opinions and Behavior Across Cultures in San Antonio*. Occasional paper no. 5. San Antonio, TX: Southwest Voter Registration Project.

Brittain, Jack W., and Douglas R. Wholey. 1988. "Competition and Coexistence in Organizational Communities: Population Dynamics in Electronic Components Manufacturing." In *Ecological Models of Organizations*, edited by Glenn R. Carroll. Cambridge, MA: Ballinger.

Browning, Rufus, Dale Marshall, and David Tabb. 1990. *Racial Politics in American Cities*. New York: Longman Press.

Buechler, Steven. 1990. *Women's Movements in the United States: Women Suffrage, Equal Rights, and Beyond*. New Brunswick, NJ: Rutgers University Press.

Byron, William, with the assistance of John D. McCarthy. 1989. "Empowerment and Progress in the Campaign for Human Development." *America*, April 15, 350-352.

Campaign for Human Development. 1989. *Catalog of Technical Assistance Providers*. Washington, DC: United States Conference of Catholic Bishops.

Carden, Maren. 1978. "The Proliferation of a Social Movement." *Social Movement Conflict and Change* 1:179-196.

Carson, Clayborne. 1981. *In Struggle: SNCC and the Black Awakening of the 1960s*. Cambridge, MA: Harvard University Press.

Castells, Manuel. 1977. *The Urban Question*. London, England: Edward Arnold.

___. 1978. *City, Class, and Power*. New York, NY: St. Martin's Press.

___. 1983. *The City and the Grassroots*. London, England: Edward Arnold.

Center for Community Change. 1989. *Community Reinvestment Act: A Citizens Action Guide*. Washington DC: Center for Community Change.

Clavel, Pierre, and Wim Wiewel. 1991. *Harold Washington and the Neighborhoods*. New Brunswick, NJ: Rutgers University Press.

Cohen, Jean. 1985. "Strategy or Identity: New Theoretical Paradigms and Contemporary Social Movements." *Social Research* 52:663-716.

Coleman, James. 1982. The Asymmetric Society. Syracuse: Syracuse University Press.

___. 1986a. *Individual Interests and Collective Action*. Cambridge, MA: Harvard University Press.

___. 1986b. "Social Theory, Social Research, and a Theory of Action." *American Journal of Sociology* 91:1309-1335.

Conell, Carol, and Kim Voss. 1990. "Formal Organization and the Fate of Social Movements: Craft Association and Class Alliance in the Knights of Labor." *American Sociological Review* 55:255-269.

Dahl, Robert. 1967. *Pluralist Democracy in the United States*. Chicago: Rand McNally.

Darden, Joe, Richard Hill, June Thomas, and Richard Thomas. 1987. *Detroit: Race and Uneven Development*. Philadelphia: Temple University Press.

Davis, John. 1991. *Contested Ground*. Ithaca, NY: Cornell University Press.

Delgado, Gary. 1986. *Organizing the Movement: The Roots and Growth of ACORN*. Philadelphia: Temple University Press.

___. 1991. Interview by author, May. Oakland, CA.

DiMaggio, Paul. 1988. "Interest and agency in institutional theory." In *Institutional Patterns and Organizations: Culture and Environment*, edited by Lynne Zucker. Cambridge, MA: Ballinger.

DiMaggio, Paul, and Walter W. Powell. 1983. "The Iron Cage Revisited: Institutional Isomorphism and Collective Rationality in Organizational Fields." *American Sociological Review* 48:147-160.

Donovan, John. 1973. *The Politics of Poverty*. Indianapolis, IN: Bobbs-Merrill.

Dulles, Foster Rhea, and Melvyn Dubofsky. 1984. *Labor in America: A History*. Arlington Heights, IL: Harlan Davidson.

Eisinger, Peter. 1973. "The Conditions of Protest Behavior in American Cities." *American Political Science Review* 67:11-28.

Everett, Kevin D. 1992. "Opening Doors for Change: Movement Funding and Organizational Transformation." Paper delivered at the annual meetings of the American Sociological Association, Pittsburgh, PA. August.

Fisher, Robert. 1984. *Let the People Decide: Neighborhood Organizing in America*. Boston: Twayne Publishers.

Freeman, Jo. 1973. "The Origins of the Women's Liberation Movement." *American Journal of Sociology* 4:792-811.

___. 1977. "Resource Mobilization and Strategy: A Model for Analyzing SMO Actions." In *The Dynamics of Social Movements*, edited by M. Zald and J. McCarthy. Lanham, MD: University Press of America.

Gamson, William. 1990a. "The Social Psychology of Collective Action." Paper delivered at the 1990 American Sociological Association Meetings. Washington, DC. August.

___. 1990b. *The Strategy of Social Protest*. Belmont, CA: Wadsworth.

Georgakas, Dan, and Marvin Surkin. 1975. *Detroit: I Do Mind Dying*. New

York: St. Martin's Press.

Gerth, Hans, and C. Wright Mills. 1946. *From Max Weber: Essays in Sociology*. New York: Oxford University Press.

Geschwender, James. 1967. "Continuities in Theories of Status Consistency and Cognitive Dissonance." *Social Forces* 46:165-167.

Gillespie, David. 1983. "Conservative Tactics in Social Movement Organizations." In *Social Movements of the Sixties and Seventies*, edited by Jo Freeman. New York: Longman.

Gills, Doug. 1991. "Chicago Politics and Community Development: A Social Movement Perspective." In *Harold Washington and the Neighborhoods*, edited by P. Clavel and W. Wiewel. New Brunswick, NJ: Rutgers University Press.

Goldstone, Jack. 1980. "The Weakness of Organization: A New Look at Gamson's *The Strategy of Social Protest*." *American Journal of Sociology* 85:1017-1043.

Gusfield, Joseph. 1963. *Symbolic Crusade: Status Politics and the American Temperance Movement*. Urbana: University of Illinois Press.

Habermas, Jurgen. 1975. *Legitimation Crisis*. Translated by T. McCarthy. Boston: Beacon Press.

___. 1984. *The Theory of Communicative Action*. Translated by T. McCarthy. Boston: Beacon Press.

Hall, Melvin F. 1991. "The Goal is to Win: Poor People's Social Movement Organizations and Collective Action." Paper delivered at the 1991 annual meetings of the American Sociological Association. Cincinnati, OH. August.

Hall, Melvin F., and Leda McIntyre Hall. 1993. "A Growth Machine for Those Who Count." *Critical Sociology* 20:79-101.

Hannan, Michael, and John Freeman. 1977. "The Population Ecology of Organizations." *American Journal of Sociology* 82:929-964.

___. 1989. *Organizational Ecology*. Cambridge: Harvard Press.

Healey, Paul. 1979. "A Banker's Guide to the Community Reinvestment Act." *Banking Law Journal* 96:705-37.

Helfgot, Joseph. 1974. "Professional Reform Organizations and the Symbolic Representation of the Poor." *American Sociological Review* 39:475-491.

Hertz, Susan. 1981. *The Welfare Mothers Movement: A Decade of Change*. Washington, DC: University Press of America.

Holler, Tom. 1991. Lead organizer for Citizens Organized for Public Service, San Antonio, Interview by the author. San Antonio, TX. August.

"Home Mortgage Disclosure." 1989. Federal Register 54:51357-51371.

Horwitt, Sanford D. 1989. *Let Them Call Me Rebel: Saul Alinsky, His Life and Legacy*. New York: Knopf.

House, Robert J. 1988. "Power and Personality in Complex Organizations."
    In *Research in Organizational Behavior*, edited by Barry M. Staw
    and L. L. Cummings. Greenwich, CT: JAI Press, Inc.

Imig, Douglas. 1992. "Resource Mobilization and Survival Tactics of
    Poverty Advocacy Groups." *Western Political Quarterly* 45:501-520.

Inglehart, Ronald. 1971. "The Silent Revolution in Europe: Intergenerational
    Change in Post-Industrial Societies." *American Political Science
    Review* 65:991-1017.

Jacobs, Bruce. 1981. *The Political Economy of Organizational Change:
    Quantitative Studies in Social Relations*. New York: Academic
    Press.

Jencks, Christopher. 1992. *Rethinking Social Policy: Race, Poverty and the
    Underclass*. Cambridge, MA: Harvard University Press.

Jenkins, J. Craig. 1981. "Sociopolitical Movements." In *Handbook of
    Political Science*, edited by S. Long. New York: Plenum Press.

___. 1983. "Resource Mobilization Theory and the Study of Social
    Movements." *Annual Review of Sociology* 9:527-550.

___. 1985a. "Foundation Funding of Progressive Social Movements." In
    Grants Seekers Guide, edited by Jill R. Shellow. Mt. Kisco, NY:
    Moyer Bell Limited.

___. 1985b. *The Politics of Insurgency*. New York: Columbia University
    Press.

Jenkins, J. Craig, and David Eckert. 1986. "Channeling Black Insurgency:
    Elite Patronage and Professional Social Movement Organizations in
    the Development of the Black Movement." *American Sociological
    Review* 51:812-829.

Jenkins, J. Craig, and Charles Perrow. 1977. "Insurgency of the Powerless:
    Farm Worker Movements, 1946-1972." *American Sociological
    Review* 42:249-268.

Jennings, James. 1986. *Daring to Seek Justice: The Story of the Campaign for
    Human Development*. Washington, DC: U.S. Catholic Conference
    Office of Publishing.

Johnson, David, John Booth, and Richard Harris. 1983. *The Politics of San
    Antonio*. Lincoln: University of Nebraska Press.

Jones, Bryan, and Lynn Bachelor. 1986. *The Sustaining Hand: Community
    Leadership and Corporate Power*. Lawrence: University of Kansas
    Press.

Kahn, Si. 1982. *Organizing: A Guide for Grassroots Leaders*. New York:
    McGraw-Hill.

Katz, Daniel, and Robert L. Kahn. 1978. *The Social Psychology of
    Organizations*. New York: Wiley.

Kaus, Mickey. 1992. *The End of Equality*. New York: Basic Books.

Klandermans, Bert. 1984. "Mobilization and Participation: Social-

Psychological Expansions of Resource Mobilization Theory." *American Sociological Review* 49:583-600.

___. 1986. "New Social Movements and Resource Mobilization: The European and the American Approach." *Journal of Mass Emergencies and Disasters* 4:13-38.

Klandermans, Bert, and Sidney Tarrow. 1988. "Mobilization into Social Movements: Synthesizing European and American Approaches." In *International Social Movement Research: From Structure to Action, Comparing Social Movement Research Across Cultures*, edited by Bert Klandermans, Hanspeter Kriesi, and Sidney Tarrow. Greenwich, CT: JAI Press.

Knoke, David. 1990. *Organizing for Collective Action*. Hawthorne, NY: Gruyter.

Kornhauser, William. 1959. *Politics of Mass Society*. Glencoe, IL: The Free Press.

LaFrance, Mayo, and Marianne LaFrance. 1977. *Evaluating Research in Social Psychology: A Guide for the Consumer*. Monterey, CA: Brooks and Cole.

Lang, Kurt, and Gladys Lang. 1961. *Collective Dynamics*. New York: Thomas Crowell Co.

Langton, Nancy. 1986. "Niche Theory and Social Movement: A Population Ecology Approach." *Sociological Quarterly* 28:51-70.

Le Bon, Gustav. 1897. *The Crowd*. London: T. Fischer University.

Lehman, Nicholas. 1991. *The Promised Land*. New York: A. A. Knopf.

Lineberry, Robert, and Edmund Fowler. 1967. "Reformism and Public Policies in American Cities." *American Political Science Review* 61:710-725.

Lipsky, Michael. 1968. "Protest as a Political Resource." *American Political Science Review* 62:1144-1158.

McAdam, Douglas. 1982. *Political Process and the Development of Black Insurgency, 1930-1970*. Chicago: University of Chicago Press.

___. 1989. "The Biographical Consequences of Activism." *American Sociological Review* 54:744-760.

McCarthy, John D. 1993. Telephone interview by the author. May.

McCarthy, John D., David W. Britt, and Mark Wolfson. 1991. "The Institutional Channeling of Social Movements by the State in the United States." *Research in Social Movements, Conflicts and Change* 13:45-76.

McCarthy, John D., Joseph Shields and Ann Patrick Conrad. 1988. *The Campaign for Human Developement: Strategic Planning and Process Reports*. Washington DC: Campaign for Human Development.

McCarthy, John and Mayer Zald. 1973. *The Trend of Social Movements in America: Professionalization and Resource Mobilization*.

Morristown, NJ: General Learning Press.

___. 1977. "Resource Mobilization and Social Movements: A Partial Theory." *American Journal of Sociology* 82:1212-1241.

McIntyre Hall, Leda, and Melvin F. Hall. 1993. "Detroit's Urban Regime: Composition and Consequence." *Mid-American Review of Sociology* 17:19-37.

Marwell, Gerald, Pamela Oliver, and Richard Prahl. 1988. "Social Networks and Collective Action: A Theory of the Critical Mass." *American Journal of Sociology* 94:502-534.

Marx, Gary. 1969. *Protest and Prejudice*. New York: Harper and Row.

Marx, Gary, and Douglas McAdam. 1994. *Collective Behavior and Social Movements*. Englewood Cliffs, NJ: Prentice-Hall.

Marx, Gary and J. Wood. 1975. "Strands of Theory and Research in Collective Behavior." *Annual Review of Sociology* 1:363-428.

Melucci, Albert. 1989. *Nomads of the Present*. Philadelphia: Temple University Press.

Meyer, John W., and Brian Rowan. 1977. "Institutional Organizations: Formal Structure as Myth and Ceremony." *American Journal of Sociology* 83:340-363.

Michels, Robert. 1949. *Political Parties*. Glencoe, IL: Free Press.

Miller, Char, and Heywood Sanders. 1990. *Urban Texas*. College Station: Texas A & M University Press.

Miller, Randall, and George Pozzetta. 1988. *Shades in the Sunbelt: Essays on Ethnicity, Race, and the Urban South*. New York: Greenwood Press.

Mills, C. Wright. 1959. *The Power Elite*. New York: Oxford University Press.

Milofsky, Carl. 1988. "Structure and Process in Community Self-Help Organizations." *Community Organizations: Studies in Resource Mobilization and Change*. New York: Oxford University Press.

Mohl, Raymond. 1988. "Ethnic Politics in Miami." In *Shades in the Sunbelt: Essays on Ethnicity, Race, and the Urban South*, edited by R. Miller and G. Pozzetta. New York: Greenwood Press.

Morris, Aldon. 1984. *The Origins of the Civil Rights Movement: Black Communities Organizing For Change*. New York: Free Press.

Moynihan, Daniel P. 1969. *Maximum Feasible Misunderstanding*. New York: Free Press.

Munoz, Carlos, and Charles Henry. 1990. "Coalition Politics in San Antonio and Denver: The Cisneros and Pena Mayoral Campaigns." In *Racial Politics in American Cities*, edited by Rufus Browning, Dale Marshall, and David Tabb. New York: Longman Press.

Murray, Charles. 1984. *Losing Ground: American Social Policy, 1950-1980*. New York: Basic Books.

National Conference of Catholic Bishops. 1969. *Resolution on Crusade against Poverty.* Washington, DC: The United States Catholic Conference.

Nix, Harold. 1976. "Concepts of Community and Community Leadership." In *Leadership and Social Change*, edited by William Lassey and Richard Fernandez, LaJolla, CA: University Associates.

Oberschall, Anthony. 1973. *Social Conflict and Social Movements.* Englewood, NJ: Prentice-Hall.

___. 1993. *Social Movements.* New Brunswick, NJ: Transaction Publishers.

Oliver, Christine. 1991. "Strategic Responses to Institutional Processes." *Academy of Management Review* 16:145-179.

Oliver, Pamela. 1988. "The Theory of Critical Mass: The Paradox of Group Size in Collective Action." *American Sociological Review* 53:1-8.

Oliver, Pamela, and Gerald Marwell. 1992. "Mobilizing Technologies for Collective Action." In *Frontiers in Social Movement Theory*, edited by Aldon D. Morris and Carol McClurg Mueller. New Haven, CT: Yale University Press.

Olson, Mancur. 1965. *The Logic of Collective Action.* Cambridge, MA: Harvard University Press.

Olzak, Susan. 1989. "Analysis of Events in the Study of Collective Action." *Annual Review of Sociology* 15:119-141.

Patterson, James T. 1981. *American's Struggle Against Poverty, 1900-1980.* Cambridge, MA: Harvard University Press.

Perin, Constance. 1977. *Everything in Its Place: Social Order and Land Use in America.* Princeton, NJ: Princeton University Press.

Perrow, Charles. 1979. *Complex Organizations, A Critical Essay.* 2d ed. Palo Alto, CA: Scott, Foresman.

Perry, Cynthia. 1990. *IAF: 50 Years Organizing for Change.* San Francisco: Sapir Press.

Petras, James, and Maurice Zeitland. 1967. "Miners and Agrarian Radicalism." *American Sociological Review* 32:578-586.

Pfeffer, Jeffrey, and Huseyin Leblebici. 1973. "The Effect of Competition on Some Dimensions of Organizational Structure." *Social Forces* 52:268-279.

Piven, Francis F., and Richard Cloward. 1977. *Poor People's Movements.* New York: Vintage Books.

Pizzorno, Alessandro. 1978. "Political Exchange and Collective Identity in Industrial Conflict." In *The Resurgence of Class Conflict in Western Europe since 1968*, edited by C. Crouch and A. Pizzorno. London: Macmillian.

Rabinowitz, Alan. 1990. *Social Change Philanthropy in America.* New York: Quorum Books.

Rao, Hayagreeva, and Eric H. Neilsen. 1992. "An Ecology of Agency

Arrangements: Mortality of Savings and Loan Associations, 1960-1987." *Administrative Science Quarterly* 37:448-470.

Reitzes, Donald C., and Detrich C. Reitzes. 1986. "Alinsky in the 1980's: Two Contemporary Chicago Community Organizations." *Sociological Quarterly* 28:265-283.

___. 1987. *The Alinsky Legacy: Alive and Kicking*. Greenwich, CT: JAI Press.

Rogers, Mary Beth. 1991. *Cold Anger*. Denton: University of North Texas Press.

Rose, Arnold. 1967. *The Power Structure: Political Process in American Society*. New York: Oxford University Press.

Rosenthal, Naomi, and Michael Schwartz. 1989. "Spontaneity and Democracy in Social Movements." In *International Social Movement Research,* vol. 2, edited by Bert Klandermans. Greenwich, CT: JAI Press.

Sale, Kirkpatrick. 1973. *SDS*. New York: Harcourt Brace.

Schlozman, Kay Lehman, and John T. Tierney. 1986. *Organized Interests and American Democracy*. New York: Harper and Row.

Schwartz, Michael. 1976. *Radical Protest and Social Structure: The Southern Farmer's Alliance and Cotton Tenancy 1880-1890*. New York: Academic Press.

___. 1983. "Leader-Member Conflict in Protest Organizations." *Social Problems* 29:22-36.

Shields, Joseph. 1991. "The Campaign for Human Development: A Study of a Church Social Justice Activity." *Social Thought* 18:22-31.

Singh, Jitendra, David Tucker, and Robert House. 1986. "Organizational Legitimacy and the Liability of Newness." *Administrative Quarterly* 31:171-193.

Smelser, Neil. 1963. *Theory of Collective Behavior*. New York: Free Press.

Snow, David, Burke Rochford, Steven Worden, and Robert Benford. 1986. "Frame Alignment Processes, Micromobilization, and Movement Participation." *American Sociological Review* 51:464-481.

Spilerman, Seymour. 1976. "Structural Characteristics of Cities and the Severity of Racial Disorders." *American Sociological Review* 41:771-793.

Staber, Udo H. 1992. "Organizational Interdependence and Organization Mortaility in the Cooperative Sector: A Community Ecology Perspective." *Human Relations* 45:1191-1212.

Staggenborg, Suzanne. 1989. Organizational and Environmental Influences on the Development of the Pro-Choice Movement." *Social Forces* 68:204-240.

Stark, Margaret, Walter Raine, Stephen Burbeck, and Keith Davison. 1974. "Some Empirical Patterns in a Riot Process." *American Sociological*

Review 39:865-876.

Starks, Robert, and Michael Preston. 1990. "Harold Washington and the Politics of Reform in Chicago." In *Racial Politics in American Cities*, edited by Rufus Browning, Dale Marshall, and David Tabb. New York: Longman Press.

Tarrow, Sidney. 1988a. *Democracy and Disorder: Social Conflict, Political Protest and Democracy in Italy: 1966-1973*. Ithaca, NY: Cornell University Press.

___. 1988b. "National Politics and Collective Action: Recent Theory and Research in Western Europe and the United States." *Annual Review of Sociology* 14:421-440.

Tilly, Charles. 1978. *From Mobilization to Revolution*. New York: Random House.

___. 1985. "Models and Realities of Popular Collective Action." *Social Research* 52:717-747.

Tilly, Charles, Louise Tilly, and Richard Tilly. 1975. *The Rebellious Century*. Cambridge, MA: Harvard University Press.

Touraine, Alain. 1981. *The Voice and the Eye*. Translated by Alan Duff. London: Cambridge University Press.

___. 1983. with François Dubet, Michel Wieviorka, and Jan Strzelecki. *Solidarity: Poland 1980-81*. Cambridge: Cambridge University Press.

___. 1984. *Return of the Actor*. Translated by Myrna Godzich. Minneapolis: University of Minnesota Press.

Turner, Ralph and Lewis Killian. 1957. *Collective Behavior*. Englewood Cliffs, NJ: Prentice-Hall, Inc.

United States Catholic Conference (USCC). 1986. *Daring to Seek Justice, People Working Together: The Story of the Campaign for Human Development, Its Roots, Its Programs and Its Challenges*. Washington, DC: USCC.

Valocchi, Steve. 1990. "The Unemployed Workers Movement of the 1930's: A Reexamination of the Piven and Cloward Thesis." *Social Problems* 37:191-205.

Walker, Jack L., Jr. 1991. *Mobilizing Interest Groups in America: Patrons, Professions, and Social Movements*. Ann Arbor: University of Michigan Press.

Walton, Hanes. 1985. *Invisible Politics: Black Political Behavior*. Albany: State University of New York Press.

Warren, Christopher, John Corbett, and John Stack. 1990. "Hispanic Ascendancy and Tripartite Politics in Miami." In *Racial Politics in American Cities*, edited by Rufus Browning, Dale Marshall, and David Tabbs. New York: Longman Press.

Weber, Max. 1947. *The Theory of Social and Economic Organization*. New

York: Oxford University Press.

West, Guida. 1981. *The National Welfare Rights Movement: The Social Protest of Poor Women*. New York: Praeger.

White, Donald. 1990. CHD field representative, Interview by the author. Washington, DC. March.

Williams, Michael R. 1985. *Neighborhood Organizations*. Westport, CT: Greenwood Press.

Wilson, John. 1973. *Introduction to Social Movements*. New York: Basic Books.

Wilson, William J. 1987. *The Truly Disadvantaged*. Chicago: University of Chicago Press.

Wylie, Jeanie. 1989. *Poletown, Community Betrayed*. Urbana: University of Illinois Press.

Zald, Mayer, and Roberta Ash. 1966. "Social Movement Organizations: Growth, Decline, and Change." *Social Forces* 44:327-40.

Zald, Mayer, and Michael Berger. 1978. "Social Movements in Organizations: Coup d'Etat, Insurgency, and Mass Movement." *American Journal of Sociology* 83:823-861.

Zald, Mayer, and Patricia Denton. 1963. "From Evangelism to General Service: On the Transformation of the YMCA." *Administrative Science Quarterly* 8:214-234.

Zald, Mayer N., and John D. McCarthy. 1987a. "Social Movement Industries: Competition and Conflict among AMOs." In *Social Movements in an Organizational Society*, edited by Mayer N. Zald and John D. McCarthy. New Brunswick, NJ: Transaction Publishers.

___. 1987b. *Social Movements in an Organizational Society*. New Brunswick, NJ: Transaction Books.

Zeitlin, Irving. 1968. *Ideology and the Development of Sociological Theory*. Englewood Cliffs, NJ: Prentice-Hall.

Zuber, Johannes, Helmut Crott, and Joachim Werner. 1992. "Choice Shift and Group Polarization: An Analysis of the Status of Arguments and Social Decision Schemes." *Journal of Personality and Social Psychology* 62:50-61.

Zurcher, Louis, and David Snow. 1981. "Collective Behavior: Social Movements." In *Social Psychology*, edited by Morris Rosenberg and Ralph H. Turner. New York: Basic Books.

Index

About the Author

MELVIN F. HALL is the director of Research and Corporate Operations for Press, Ganey Associates and an Adjunct Professor of Sociology at Indiana University, South Bend. His academic background includes extensive study of social movements. Hall was a minister and community organizer in Detroit for seven years before receiving his Ph.D. in sociology from the University of Notre Dame.